Northeast Indians

Craig A. Doherty
Katherine M. Doherty

CHELSEA HOUSE
PUBLISHERS
An imprint of Infobase Publishing

This book is dedicated to the many students of all ages we have worked with and taught over the years.

Northeast Indians
Copyright © 2008 by Craig A. Doherty and Katherine M. Doherty
Maps on pp. xi, xiii, 116,138, and 148 and image captions copyright © 2008 by Infobase Publishing
Maps on pp. 2, 3, 14, 19, 41, 128 © 2008 by Carl Waldman and Infobase Publishing

Chelsea House
An imprint of Infobase Publishing, Inc.
132 West 31st Street
New York NY 10001

Library of Congress Cataloging-in-Publication Data
Doherty, Craig A.
    Northeast Indians / Craig A. Doherty and Katherine M. Doherty.
        p. cm. — (Native America)
    Includes bibliographical references and index.
    ISBN 978-0-8160-5968-3
  1. Indians of North America—History. 2. Indians of North America—Social life and customs. I. Doherty, Katherine M. II. Title. III. Series: Doherty, Craig A. Native America.
    E77.D66 2007
    970.004'97—dc22   2005018174

Chelsea House books are available at special discounts when purchased in bulk quantities for businesses, associations, institutions, or sales promotions. Please call our Special Sales Department in New York at (212) 967-8800 or (800) 322-8755.
You can find Chelsea House on the World Wide Web at
http://www.chelseahouse.com
Text design by Erika K. Arroyo
Cover design by Salvatore Luongo
Maps and graph by Jeremy Eagle

Printed in the United States of America
VB FOF 10 9 8 7 6 5 4 3 2 1
This book is printed on acid-free paper and contains 30% post-consumer recycled content.

➤Contents➤

⅏ Introduction ⅏

Native American peoples live and have lived for millennia throughout the Americas. Many people think of Indians solely in the past tense, as part of history. While these groups have a long and interesting history, their contributions to American society have continued through the 20th century and into the 21st century. Native America today is an exciting place, with much waiting to be discovered. This series of books will introduce readers to these cultures.

Thousands of years ago people from Asia migrated to the Western Hemisphere and spread throughout the lands that would later be called North and South America. Over the millennia, before Europeans found their way there, these peoples settled the Western Hemisphere, and a number of elaborate Native cultures developed. The Aztec, Maya, and Inca had large cities in North, Central, and South America. In what is now the United States, Pueblo groups in the Southwest and the Mound Builders in the Mississippi River basin lived in large towns and small cities. People lived in every corner of the land and adapted to every climatic condition, from the frozen Arctic home of the Inuit to the hot, dry desert inhabited by the Tohono O'odham of what is now southern Arizona and northern Mexico.

When in A.D. 1492 Christopher Columbus arrived in what Europeans would call the Americas, he mistakenly thought he was in the part of Asia known as the Indies. Columbus therefore called the people he encountered Indians. These Native Americans all had their own names for their many tribes; however, as a group they are still often referred to as American Indians or just Indians. Each group of American Indians has its own story of how its ancestors were created and ended up in the group's traditional homelands. What is known about the Americas before the arrival of Europeans, however, has been determined mainly by studying the artifacts found at archaeological sites throughout the Americas. Despite the efforts of scientists from a wide variety of fields, there remain numerous questions about how these diverse cultures developed in North America. Scholars have a number of theories.

One part of the story that most people agree on is that present-day Native peoples of the Americas—including American Indians and Inuit—are descended from those who came to America from Asia. Many came on foot before the end of the last ice age, which ended about 10,000 years ago. Others, such as the Inuit, arrived much later as they spread out around the polar ice cap by boat and over the ice. Many sources refer to a "land bridge" that existed between what is now Siberia and Alaska and allowed the passage of people from Asia to North America. In many ways, this is a misleading term. During the last ice age, from about 40,000 years ago to 10,000 years ago, large sheets of ice called glaciers that were thousands of feet thick at times extended into North America as far as what is now the northern part of the United States. There was so much water locked into the glaciers that scientists estimate that the oceans were more than 400 feet lower than they are today.

The Bering Sea is the body of water that now lies between Siberia and Alaska. However, 400 feet beneath this sea is a land mass more than 1,000 miles wide. So, instead of talking about a

THE STUDY OF PALEO-INDIANS

Scientists from a variety of fields have worked to explain the origins of the more than 500 tribes that existed in North America at the end of the 15th century. The people who play the biggest role in this research are archaeologists. An archaeologist studies the past by finding objects called artifacts that people leave behind. Archaeologists refer to the earliest people in North America as Paleo-Indians. They use this term because they are studying people who lived during the Paleolithic period, or Old Stone Age, which existed from about 40,000 to 10,000 years ago in North America.

In addition to archaeologists digging up artifacts to study, other scientists contribute information about the plants, animals, climate, and geologic conditions that existed at the time. Still other scientists have developed numerous techniques to date the artifacts that the archaeologists dig up.

historical, narrow "land bridge" that facilitated the peopling of the Americas, it is important to see the area that scientists now refer to as Beringia as a wide, relatively flat plain that looked

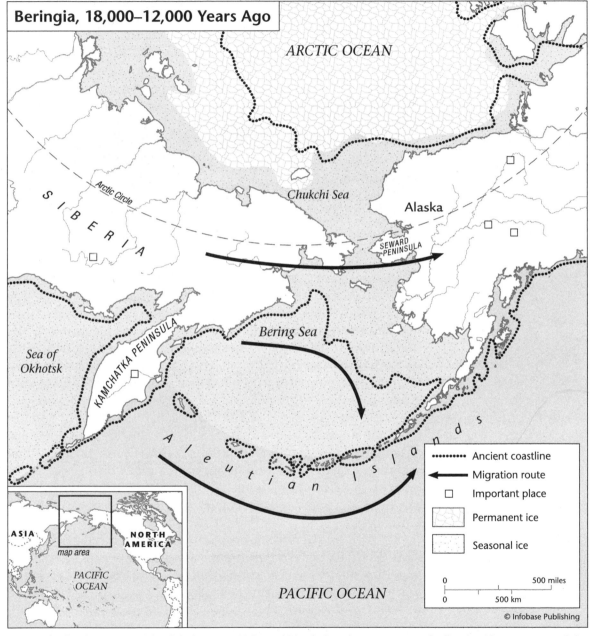

During the last ice age a wide plain between Asia and North America was exposed, allowing the ancestors of the American Indians to cross to the Americas. These first Americans traveled over land and across the seasonal sea ice that formed along the shoreline. Scientists refer to this area as Beringia, as it is now under the Bering Sea.

Glaciers, such as the one pictured here in the mountains of British Columbia, once covered most of the northern part of North America. *(Library of Congress, Prints and Photographs Division [LC-D4-14664])*

like the treeless tundra that still exists in the far north. Starting 25,000 years ago, or some would argue even earlier, bands of Paleolithic hunter-gatherers, people who lived by hunting animals and gathering wild plants, crossed Beringia, and the ice along its shores, to North America.

These first ancestors of the American Indians hunted many different animals that are now extinct. During this long ice age, many large mammals known as megafauna existed. They included mastodons, wooly mammoths, giant bison, and other large plant-eaters. There were also large predators such as American lions and saber-toothed tigers. The bones of many of these animals have been dug up at the campsites of Paleo-Indians.

Geologists, scientists who study the origins and changes in Earth's surface, believe that there was a period of time more than 23,000 years ago when people could have traveled down the Pacific coast. After that, the glaciers made it impossible for people to move south or to cross them. Then about 14,000 years ago, the coastal route was again open enough for migration. Approximately 11,500 years ago, the glacier in North America had melted to the point that there were two separate areas of ice. In the

West, much of the area from the mountains along the Pacific coast to the Rocky Mountains was covered by what is known as the Cordilleran ice sheet. In the East, ice covered the land in a continuous sheet from the Arctic Ocean south into what is today New England, New York, Ohio, Michigan, Wisconsin, Minnesota, and North and South Dakota. This is known as the Laurentide ice sheet. Between the two areas of glacier, there was an ice-free corridor from Alaska south into what is now the central plains of the United States. Many scientists agree that when this corridor opened, Paleo-Indians spread through the Americas.

Although most scientists agree on the major overland migration routes from Asia, some have suggested that Paleo-Indians may also have traveled down the Pacific coast of both North

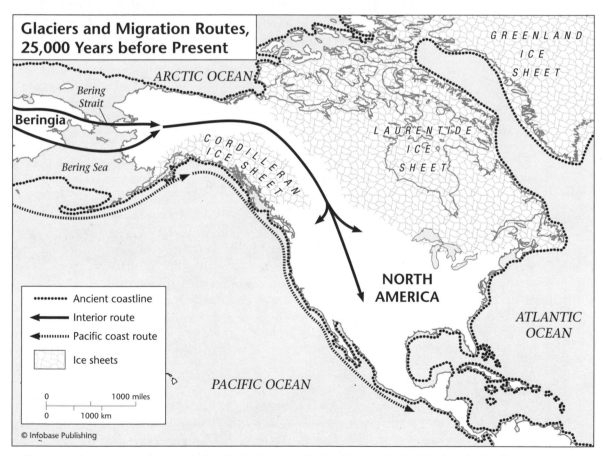

At first, people migrating from Asia lived in Beringia and what is now Alaska. As the glaciers began to melt, people were able to move south. The route along the Pacific coast opened up first, and then an ice-free area existed down through the North American plains.

and South America. They believe that boats may have been used by people who reached South America during these paleo-migrations. The fact that at least one site in southern Chile has been dated to at least 12,500 years ago would suggest that bands of people had spread out in the Americas well before the major migrations that appear to have taken place 11,500 years ago. The modern study of genetics has created speculation that one other possible route of migration existed during the Paleolithic period. Approximately 3 percent of American Indians share a genetic trait that is also found in parts of Europe. This has led to the idea that some people may have come from Europe by boat during Paleolithic times.

Most of what is believed about Paleo-Indians is very speculative because there are very few artifacts that have been found from these earliest Americans. It is now accepted, however, that as the glaciers receded, people spread through the Americas. They lived by hunting and gathering. It was once widely believed that these people lived primarily by hunting

Large animals known as megafauna, such as the wooly mammoth pictured here, roamed North America during the last ice age and were hunted by Paleo-Indians. (© Science VU/Visuals Unlimited)

STONE TOOLS

Although in some areas of North America the American Indians made tools and decorative objects out of copper and the Inuit were known to make knives out of iron from recovered meteorites, the vast majority of tools were made of stone. Knives used for cutting, points for spears and arrows, as well as small blades and scrapers used in a variety of tasks were all made by flaking off pieces of a variety of types of stones. Flint, chert, and obsidian are all types of rock that flake apart when struck.

To make stone tools, the toolmaker started with a large piece of rock and hit it with a rock hammer. Large flakes of stone would break off and then be broken into smaller usable shapes and sizes. To remove smaller and smaller pieces as the tool was shaped and sharpened, different methods were applied. Often the toolmaker would use the point of an antler to apply pressure to a specific spot on the stone to remove a flake. Sometimes the antler was struck with a piece of wood until a flake of stone was removed. Other toolmakers applied pressure to the antler tip until the flake came off. As the edge took shape, smaller and smaller pieces were removed until the edge was extremely sharp. If the edge became dull, it could be reworked to sharpen it. The sites where usable stone is found often show that they were mined by Native Americans for thousands of years, going back to Paleo-Indian times.

large animals such as the wooly mammoth and the giant bison. Although there are many archaeological sites that contain the bones of these large animals, it is now thought that these people also hunted many smaller animals and gathered the edible parts of many wild plants.

The original weapons of these early American Indians consisted of wooden spears with tips that had been hardened with fire. Some time after people were able to use the migration route in the center of North America, they began to attach stone points onto their spears. It is by the size and style of these stone points that archaeologists have been able to identify and group people into a number of paleocultural groups.

As archaeologists discovered early sites of human occupation in North America, they noticed that different groups used different shaped tools. These groups were usually named after the location of the sites where their artifacts were first found. Three of these earliest groups were first discovered in New Mexico, and one was found in Texas. Evidence of the New Mexico groups was first found near the towns of Clovis and Folsom, and the third group was found in the Sandia Mountains east of Albuquerque. The fourth group was first discovered near Plainview,

Clovis-style stone spear points are found in many locations throughout North America, indicating a relationship between early hunter-gatherer groups. *(Photo courtesy of Pete Bostrom)*

Texas, and is referred to as the Plano culture. Each of these groups had its own unique style of making their stone spear points; therefore, archaeologists can easily identify a Clovis- or Folsom-style spear point wherever it is found.

As the glaciers continued to recede, the people of these groups spread out in search of animals to hunt and plants to gather. Clovis-style spear points have been found throughout much of North America, and at one time scientists believed the Clovis people were the first North Americans. It is now known that the earliest Clovis sites date to about 11,500 years ago and that people were in the Americas long before that. Some people suggest that the Clovis people were a new wave of migration into the Americas. Others think that they had been in Alaska for a long time and moved south about this time as travel became possible down the center of North America. It may never be known which theories are accurate.

What is known for certain is that these early culture groups in the center of the continent spread east, west, and south. It is also known that the climate began to change. Between 10,000 and 5,000 B.C., North America went from the Ice Age with its large Pleistocene (time period from 1.6 million to 10,000 years ago) animals, like the saber-toothed tiger and wooly mammoth, to the climate and landscape that exists today. The Paleo-Indians that existed at the beginning of this time learned from generation to generation to adapt to changes in their environment.

Over thousands of years between the end of the last ice age and the coming of Europeans to North America, the different cultures of American Indians developed along a number of lines. As the climate became less severe, American Indians spread out to cover the entire continent. They created new technologies to deal with the vastly different environments that they encountered. By the end of this time, the American Indians had broken into distinct language groups and eventually into a wide variety of tribes.

Modern researchers divided North America, excluding Mexico, into 10 cultural regions, known as culture areas, to aid in their study of American Indians. In classifying these areas, scientists took many factors into account. Among those were similarity in culture, environment, and geography. Within a culture area there may be a number of tribes that speak languages that differ, however, the way they have adapted to the geography of the region gave groups many similarities. For example, in the California Culture Area almost all groups used acorns as a major source of food. Therefore, they all had similar technology for harvesting, processing, cooking, and preserving acorns. In the Plateau Culture Area the prolific runs of salmon in the many rivers of the region became the primary food source and focus of the culture. Each of the ten regions has similar unifying aspects.

In some of these culture areas, however, there are numerous distinctions that can be made between groups in the region. For instance, in the Southwest, two distinct cultures live side by side within one culture area. One group known as Pueblo Indians (*pueblo* is the Spanish word for "town") lived in towns and were primarily farmers: Others consisted of various groups, such as

Acoma Pueblo in New Mexico is the oldest continuously inhabited community in the United States. Pueblo people have lived in Acoma for more than 1,000 years. *(Library of Congress, Prints and Photographs Division [LC-USZ62-74105])*

During World War II, the U.S. Army recruited members of the Navajo (Dineh) tribe to create a code using Navajo to transmit sensitive messages. This code proved indecipherable to enemies. *(Official U.S. Marine Corps photo USMC #69896/National Archives and Records Administration)*

the related Navajo (Dineh) and Apache, who were seminomadic and depended much more on hunting and gathering than on agriculture. In this region, the unifying aspect is more closely related to geography and climate of the region.

The culture areas that most scientists agree on are the Northeast, Southeast, Great Plains, Great Basin, Plateau, Southwest, California, Northwest Coast, Subarctic, and Arctic. Each volume in this series will show how the peoples in a culture area developed their distinct way of life, making the transition from Ice Age hunters/gatherers to the complex tribal cultures that existed when Christopher Columbus landed in the Caribbean in 1492. The lifeways and material culture of these people will be described in depth. Spiritual beliefs and social structure are also explained. Furthermore, readers will learn of the wide variety of housing and transportation developed for each region. Clothing and everyday items will be described, as will hunting, fishing, farming, and cooking practices. Readers will also learn how the American Indians fought to survive the long invasion of European settlers that followed Columbus and explore how, despite the best attempts of Europeans to eliminate the American Indians almost everywhere they found them, many tribes persevered and continue to exist today.

The long and fascinating history of Indian peoples is described, illuminating the many contributions made by Indians and Indian cultures to the broader American culture. In the 20th century, Indians finally began to have some success in regaining some land and respect. Indian soldiers fought bravely in various wars the United States participated in. All American Indians finally gained citizenship. Protests starting in the 1950s and 1960s as well as the work of Indian leaders resulted in victories in the courts and legislative chambers of North America. Increased pride in their heritage and a resurgence of Indian cultures have given many American Indians an optimistic outlook for the future as the 21st century unfolds.

Stone Age Hunters to Woodland Indians

The region in which peoples of the Northeast Culture Area live is very large. It stretches north to south from the Saint Lawrence River Valley in Canada to North Carolina and Tenncssee. It extends east to Cape Breton Island in Nova Scotia and west to the Mississippi River valley. Within this vast region with numerous climates and ecologies were many differences in the traditional lifestyles of people who lived along the Atlantic coast and its numerous estuaries, on the Great Lakes, or in the interior of New England. There are a number of tribes who speak a variety of languages in the Northeast. However, despite the differences, the Indians of the Northeast are much more similar than they are different.

Anthropologists, scientists who study the way people live, refer to the Indians of the Northeast as Woodland Indians, because they traditionally depended on the forests of the region to satisfy many of their needs. By the time Europeans began visiting the coast of Canada and the United States in the 16th century, the Indians of the Northeast had a diverse lifestyle that include farming, hunting, gathering, and fishing. There was also extensive trade and interaction between the tribes throughout the region. The civilization the Europeans found had developed over thousands of years.

PALEO-INDIANS
(Approximately 10,500–6000 B.C.)

When the first people came to North America, most of the Northeast region was covered with ice. This prevented Paleo-Indians

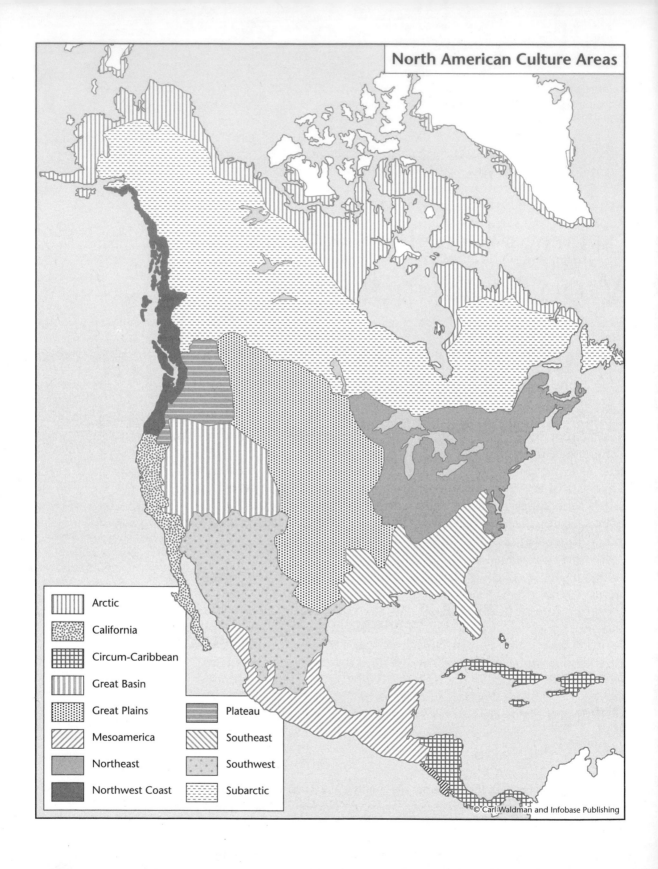

North American Culture Areas

Arctic

California

Circum-Caribbean

Great Basin

Great Plains

Mesoamerica

Northeast

Northwest Coast

Plateau

Southeast

Southwest

Subarctic

© Carl Waldman and Infobase Publishing

(opposite page) Scientists have divided North America into 12 Indian culture areas. Ten of these areas are at least partially in the United States and are included in this series. The American Indians who lived in each area shared a number of cultural similarities.

from entering the area until after the glaciers began to melt around 12,500 B.C. In the very southern extent of the region, at Meadowcroft Rockshelter (a cave in modern-day Pennsylvania), scientists have used geochronological and radiocarbon techniques to date artifacts to some time between 14,225 and 11,300 B.C. Archaeologists have yet to associate these artifacts with any of the later culture groups. The majority of the Paleo-Indian sites

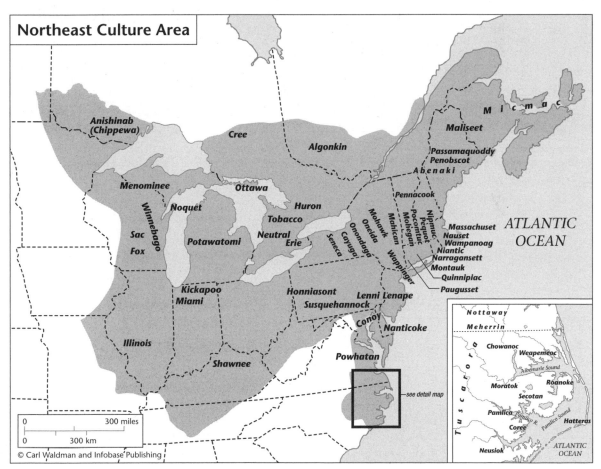

This map shows many of the numerous tribes in the Northeast Culture Area and places them where they lived before the coming of Europeans to North America. The Indians of the Northeast depended on the forests around them for many of their needs and are therefore referred to as Woodland Indians.

At the Meadowcroft Rockshelter in Pennsylvania, scientists have dated artifacts to between 14,225 and 11,300 B.C., indicating they were left behind by Paleo-Indians. *(Courtesy of Francesca DiPietro Bowman)*

in the Northeast have Clovis-like spear points and have been dated to sometime between 10,500 and 8000 B.C.

How the Paleo-Indians of the Northeast lived has been reconstructed based on the data from numerous archaeological sites. Throughout the area, sites have produced similar artifacts that include stone tools and other items of daily life. The bones of various animals, including birds and fish, indicate that these Paleo-Indians hunted everything from megafauna, or very large animals, such as wooly mammoths, to much smaller animals, such as turtles and rabbits. As the climate changed throughout this period, the megafauna became extinct and the hunters depended more and more on the animals that are familiar today in the Northeast. Where they were plentiful, the white-tailed deer, caribou, bison, and moose all became important sources of food. There is also evidence that the Paleo-Indians gathered the produce of many different plants to supplement their diet of wild game.

DATING ARTIFACTS

Scientists use a number of methods to determine the age of an archaeological site. One of the most common is the carbon-14 method. All living organisms have a known amount of carbon-14 molecules. When the organism dies, carbon 14 begins to disintegrate at a rate that is also known. By measuring the amount of carbon 14 in a piece of wood uncovered at an archaeological site, scientists can tell when that wood was cut from a living tree, giving an approximate date for the site. Although conditions of the material and the site can cause a certain amount of error, carbon-14 dating is very important in determining a site's age.

Scientists use other methods as well. The depth and number of layers of sediment at a site can help a geologist determine how long ago an artifact was left at a site. This method is called geochronology. To date more recent sites, scientists have developed a time line based on the pattern created by the growth rings of certain types of trees. This is referred to as dendrochronology. By overlapping a large number of samples, they have been able to extend the dendrochronological time line back almost 4,000 years. Scientists can also tell when an obsidian stone tool was made by measuring the amount of moisture that has escaped from the stone. This is known as obsidian hydration dating.

Paleo-Indians most likely lived in small bands that worked together to provide food for the group. They often lived in caves or places where there were rock overhangs that gave them shelter from the weather. Many of these rock shelters have been discovered to contain numerous artifacts from thousands of years of use. It is believed that these people also constructed shelters of brush when they could not find an adequate cave or rock shelter. As the climate and ecology of the Northeast reached its current state about 5,000 years ago, the lifestyle of the Indians of the area began to change.

EARLY ARCHAIC PERIOD
(6000–3000 B.C.)

Archaeologists have determined that starting about 6000 B.C. there was a change in the artifacts left at sites. New forms of tools, for example, separate the Paleo-Indian period from what is referred to as the Archaic period. There are some conflicting ideas

As the climate in North America changed, the Indians of the Northeast came to depend on large mammals such as the moose for food and hides for clothing. *(Laverne Smith/U.S. Fish and Wildlife Service)*

The abundance of deer in most of the Northeast allowed the people of the area to prosper. *(National Park Service)*

about how this change came about. Some argue that new groups moved into the area and eventually displaced the Paleo-Indians. Others suggest that the change from paleo to archaic was one of gradual transition. This latter theory suggests that the people of the Archaic period are the descendants of the Paleo-Indians of the area.

Those on both sides agree that the major cause of the transition from paleo to archaic was the changes in climate, which allowed for a large increase in population in the area. Many of the region's deciduous trees (those that lose their leaves every year) had developed edible nuts, and numerous berries had also become available at this time. Probably the

MANOS AND METATES

Throughout the Americas, archaeologists have found a variety of stones that were used by American Indians to grind corn, nuts, and other plants that were eaten. The nuts or seeds were placed on the metate, a relatively flat or grooved stone. The mano, a smaller stone, was held in the hand and used to grind the plant matter against the metate. (*Mano* is the Spanish word for "hand", *metate* is also a Spanish word but borrowed from Nahuatl.) Different cultures used distinctive manos and metates, which help archaeologists identify their sites.

As corn became an important source of food for the Indians of the Northeast, different groups developed distinctive styles of manos and metates that were used to grind corn into flour. *(Library of Congress, Prints and Photographs Division [LC-USZ62-113049])*

most important change that allowed Archaic Indians to prosper, however, was the abundance of deer in the Northeast Culture Area. One of the best documented groups of the Archaic period are the people who were part of the Helton culture.

There are numerous sites in southern Illinois and Indiana that fit into the Helton culture. These people used distinctive tools and weapons that indicated they hunted, fished, and gathered food within their area. It is at sites from this time that the first manos and metates are found. Together these stones were used to grind nuts and possibly other plant matter.

The people of the Helton culture also began making a new style of dwelling. Their houses were made of wattle and daub with thatched roofs. To make this type of shelter, people wove sticks together over a frame. This was the wattle. They then coated the wattle with mud, or daub. The mud would harden to form a solid wall that kept out all but the worst weather. Large roasting pits and racks for drying fish have also been found at Helton sites. These finds have led archaeologists to believe that the people of the Helton culture tended to stay in one place more than their nomadic paleo-ancestors.

LATE ARCHAIC CULTURAL DEVELOPMENT
(3000–300 B.C.)

As the Helton culture shows the transition away from paleo lifestyles, other distinctive cultures during the next 3,000 years came and went and contributed to the slow development of the Woodland culture. The dates and locations of these transitional cultures are not exact. They often overlapped in both time and place. However, for purposes of scientific discussion they have been broken down into a number of cultural distinctions that identify them by place.

The Indians in the forests that surround the Great Lakes and the rivers that drain into it, for example, developed during this time a number of unique activities that distinguish them from other people of the Northeast. The culture that developed in this area is known as the Lake Forest culture, and its most distinguishing characteristic was the apparent emphasis on fishing. The Great Lakes and the rivers that empty into them teemed with fish, and the Lake Forest people developed unique ways of catching them. All the Indians of the Northeast at this time used hooks and lines to fish. In most cases, the hooks were made of bone, but copper hooks have been found around the western edges of the Great Lakes.

Fish hooks made of bone or copper have been found at Lake Forest culture sites around the Great Lakes. This copper fish hook was made between 5000 and 4000 B.C. *(U.S. Bureau of Ethnography)*

THE OLD COPPER CULTURE

History books often stress the importance of European metal goods to American Indians in the early days of contact between the two groups. Although it is true that most of the Indians of North America did not make tools of iron, metalworking of a variety of objects existed as early as 7,000 years ago. In what is now Wisconsin, a group known as the Old Copper culture mined deposits of pure copper, which they heated and then hammered into a variety of useful tools and decorative objects. Archaeologists have found these objects at a number of sites throughout the area, which also is an indication that trade existed at a very early time.

During the time that the Hopewell culture flourished (200 B.C.–A.D. 700), these people became extremely accomplished coppersmiths. Their tools and decorative objects are found over an even wider trading area than that of the Old Copper culture. Indians of the Northwest were known to have made large copper plates that are believed to have been objects that showed the wealth of the owners. In the Arctic, the Inuit people gathered iron from meteors and hammered it into knives and spear points.

The Lake Forest people developed additional technology for harvesting fish. Where people to their south used simple spears, the Lake Forest people developed harpoons and leisters. A harpoon is a spear with a single point, while a leister is a three-pronged spear point. The middle point stabs the fish while the points on either side hold the fish tightly until it is brought on shore. The Lake Forest people also developed seine and gill nets. A seine net is used by surrounding a school of fish and then the bottom of the net is drawn together to trap the fish. Gill nets trap fish by snaring the fish's gills in the opening in the net.

The ability of the Lake Forest people to catch and preserve large quantities of fish allowed them to prosper and expand their population. Another cultural group developed the Maritime culture along the coastal areas of northern New England and the Canadian Maritime Provinces. These people lived on a wide variety of fish and marine mammals, such as seals. Many of these people spent the spring and summer along the coast and then moved inland when the first snows came. This move was caused by two factors: First, many of the marine creatures migrated south to warmer waters in the winter, as they still do today; second, at this time, large herds of caribou came much farther south than they do today. The Indians of the Maritime culture moved along the caribou routes in the winter so that they could easily harvest these animals. The artifacts from Maritime sites in Maine and Newfoundland have led archaeologists to believe that the Maritime people became accomplished woodworkers, who probably made a variety of useful objects. A dependence on wooden objects would distinguish later Woodland Indians.

Another group in the late Archaic period was the Mixed Forest culture, which is further divided by scientists into those who lived along the Atlantic coast south of the Maritime region and those who lived in interior regions and along the large rivers of the Ohio and Mississippi River areas. Both of these groups are known to have moved seasonally to take advantage of concentrations of food within their range. In the spring, they would be along the coast and rivers to harvest fish during their annual spawning runs. In the fall, they might travel to an area that had concentrations of nuts and berries. In the winter, they would go where it was easiest to hunt for deer and other game.

During this time, the population of the Northeast grew steadily as people developed better technologies for hunting, fishing, and gathering food as well as better ways to preserve it. As the abilities to provide food for the group increased, the amount of traveling decreased. This also contributed to the development of regional differences in appearance and language.

SUSQUEHANNA TRADITION

A single technological advancement can have a huge impact on a culture. In modern times, inventions such as the automobile, telephone, and computer have all caused enormous changes in society. For the people living in the Northeast at the end of the Archaic period, the use of pottery had a similarly major impact.

Archaeologists disagree over how pottery came to be used in the Northeast. Some suggest that pottery making was introduced from the south and west. Others believe that it might have developed in the region independently. In either case, both sides agree that pottery in the Northeast was first used in the Middle Atlantic area and probably spread up the rivers of the area. One of the major rivers that empties into Chesapeake Bay is the Susquehanna that flows from central New York through Pennsylvania and into Maryland. Because the oldest use of pottery in

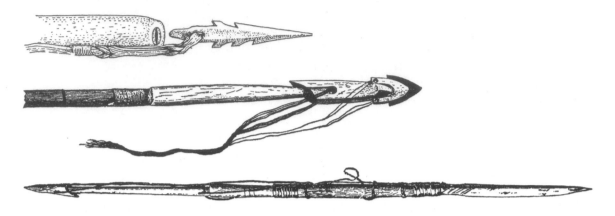

Harpoons such as those pictured here were used to spear fish. *(U.S. Bureau of Ethnography)*

the region is found along the Susquehanna River watershed, the transition from late Archaic to early Woodland culture is known as the Susquehanna tradition.

The introduction of pottery made it much easier for people to cook foods other than meat. Whereas meat could easily be grilled or cooked over an open fire, before the introduction of pottery, other foods had to be combined with water in a bark bowl. Hot stones were then placed in the bowl to cook the contents. Pottery cooking vessels, however, allowed any food to be heated directly over the fire and allowed cooks more versatility in preparing food. The people of the Susquehanna tradition who lived along the coast made other changes to their diet, such as beginning to eat large quantities of shellfish. They also made technological advances in their weapons. During this time, people began using a spear-thrower called an atlatl. With this device a hunter could throw a heavier spear faster and farther with great accuracy.

Pottery was a significant technological advancement for the people of the Susquehanna tradition. Distinctive pottery such as this Anasazi mug from the Southwest helps scientists identify archaeological sites. *(U.S. Bureau of Ethnography)*

EARLY WOODLAND CULTURE

The development of a culture is a slow process taking thousands of years. The change from late Archaic to early Woodland culture cannot be pinpointed to one time or place; however, there are the archaeological remains of groups that are significantly different from early periods and are therefore considered part of the early Woodland period. One of the first of these groups is the Adena culture (1000 B.C.–A.D. 200). The Adena culture was first identified at an archaeological site on the Adena estate near Chillicothe, Ohio, and took its name from the location of that first site.

The Indians of the Adena culture had a number of practices that were different from early groups. One distinction was the houses they built. Adena houses were circular with an outer wall made by placing posts in the ground that slanted outward. Smaller flexible poles were woven into the vertical sticks and may have been coated with mud. In the center of the circle, four tall poles were placed in the ground to support a domed roof.

The Adena people also were some of the first in the Northeast to practice agriculture. It is believed that they cultivated plants such as sunflowers, gourds, and pumpkins. They are known to have grown tobacco that was probably smoked during various ceremonies. Because of the abundance of game in their area and the beginnings of agriculture, Adena people became more sedentary, meaning they stayed in one place.

Sunflowers were grown for their oil. Some groups also pressed the ground seeds into balls that could be eaten when they traveled. *(PhotoDisc)*

Squash, including pumpkins, were one of the major crops, along with corn and beans, grown by the Indians of the Northeast. *(PhotoDisc)*

Probably the most distinctive feature of the Adena culture is the mounds they built. The Adena people constructed two primary types of mounds, one of which was burial mounds. Tombs were made of logs covered with dirt. After a number of tombs had been covered, the Adena would start another layer of tombs on top of the first layer. These burial mounds often have a low circular earthen wall around them. The other type of mound attributed to the Adena culture is effigy mounds. An effigy is a representation of a person or animal.

The most famous effigy mound of the Adena culture is the Great Serpent Mound near Peebles, Ohio. This mound is 1,348 feet long and represents a snake whose body is two to six feet high and four to 20 feet across. There is an oval object that the serpent seems to be swallowing that most believe is meant to represent an egg. Why the Adena people built this mound is unknown, but all agree that it took a large collective effort to move that much dirt and shape it into a serpent.

No one knows for sure what happened to the Adena people. By the end of their time period, they had spread over a large section of the Northeast. Scientists will probably never be sure if the Adena people left the area or were absorbed by the next early Woodland culture. Some might argue that the Hopewell culture represented the advancement of the Adena people.

The Hopewell culture (200 B.C.–A.D. 700) was centered in the Ohio and Illinois River valleys and eventually spread throughout most of the East and Midwest. The Hopewell people appear to have been the first Northeast group to have depended on agriculture. Their three primary crops—corn, beans, and squash—became the mainstay of Woodland culture.

The Great Serpent Mound near Peebles, Ohio, is 1,348 feet long and up to six feet high and 20 feet across. The purpose of the mound is not known, but it represents a huge effort on the part of the people who built it. *(Library of Congress)*

Corn

One of the greatest contributions of Native Americans to the world is corn. Around 8000 B.C., Indians in what is now Mexico began collecting the seeds from a native grass plant and cultivating them. Through careful seed selection, they transformed this grass into what is now called corn. By the time Christopher Columbus arrived in the Caribbean in A.D. 1492, Indians throughout the Americas had developed more than 700 varieties of corn. Different varieties were needed for different purposes and growing conditions. The cultivation of corn allowed American Indians to stay in one area and establish numerous complex civilizations.

There are five main types of corn. Popcorn was probably the earliest type to be developed. Its small kernels open when they are heated. Flint corn is similar to popcorn but with bigger kernels and was adapted to grow in northern climates. Flour corn is a variety that can be ground into cornmeal and used to make tortillas or cornbread. Dent corn is a variety that can be both ground into meal or used whole in soups and stews. Sweet corn is the type of corn that is usually eaten fresh as corn on the cob.

Distribution of Corn Cultivation, 1492

Cultural evidence of corn

Only archaeological evidence of corn

© Carl Waldman and Infobase Publishing

Above: The spread of corn cultivation throughout much of North America allowed many American Indians to create cultures centered on agriculture.

In addition to improved agriculture, the Hopewell culture made advances in many other areas. They built larger and more elaborate mounds. Some of their burial mounds were 40 feet high. They also built effigy mounds and mounds in complex geometric patterns. At a site near Newark, Ohio, there are the remains of walls that stood 50 feet high and were 200 feet wide at the base, covering four square miles.

Artifacts in Hopewell sites reveal their extensive trade network. Obsidian for tools has been traced back to its source in the Rocky Mountains. Copper from the Great Lakes, shells from the Gulf of Mexico and Atlantic coast, silver from Canada, and objects from other places throughout the eastern half of North America show the extent of the Hopewell trade routes. The people of the Hopewell culture also had the time to develop a number of advanced crafts.

Objects found in Hopewell burials show how talented Hopewell artists were. Carved stone pipes, ceramic figures, copper jewelry, pearls, gold objects, and numerous other beautiful artifacts are regularly found in

This engraving by Theodor de Bry based on a painting by John White records the Algonquian village of Secotan, showing its homes and crops such as corn. *(Library of Congress, Prints and Photographs Division [LC-USZ62-52444])*

Hopewell tombs. The greatest puzzle that faces scientists is the fate of the Hopewell culture. It may be that after almost 1,000 years the Hopewell culture simply faded away as other cultures have in historic and prehistoric times throughout the world. But some have speculated that the climate might have changed enough to cause crops to fail. Others suggest that war either between rival Hopewell groups or with outside groups may have been responsible for the decline of the culture.

No matter what happened to them, the Hopewell people set the stage for the Woodland Indians who inhabited the Northeast when Europeans arrived in the 16th and 17th centuries.

This human effigy pipe was excavated from a Hopewell mound in present-day Ross County, Ohio. *(The Ohio Historical Society)*

The Indians of the Northeast divided into numerous tribes and language groups, but they all shared similarities that can be first seen in the Adena and then Hopewell cultures. Over time, the Woodland Indians developed a complex lifestyle that revolved around farming and exploiting the forests around them.

Families, Clans, Tribes, and Alliances

Beginning in the 1500s, Europeans who were trying to encourage colonization portrayed North America as a vast and empty wilderness. Nothing could have been further from the truth. Although it will never be known how many people lived in the Americas in 1491, scientists are sure that the American Indians lived a rich and varied life in a land that was well known to them. They used fire extensively to clear land and maintain habitat for the animals that they depended on, such as deer. There were probably more than 500 tribes in all of North America. In the Northeast, there were more than 60 tribes that spoke a variety of languages from three major language groups.

Despite language and tribal differences, the people of the Northeast shared many cultural traits. Their religious beliefs, family and tribal organization, and way of life were all very similar. When classifying tribal groups, scientists first look at their language. The languages of the Northeast belonged to three major groups: Algonquian, Iroquoian, and Siouan. Within these groups, languages were similar, but that did not mean that distant groups could understand each other. The majority of the Northeast tribes (at least 45) spoke an Algonquian language, creating a scenario similar to the example of French and Italian. They are both from the same root language and have many similar terms, but a person speaking one cannot necessarily be understood by someone who speaks the other language. The five Iroquois tribes as well as others spoke Iroquoian languages. The Winnebago (Ho-Chunk) spoke a Siouan language.

COUNTING AMERICAN INDIANS

One of the most heated controversies among people who study the history and prehistory of American Indians is just how many of them there were in 1491. The argument revolves around this date because almost as soon as there was contact between Europeans and American Indians, the Indians began to die from conflicts with Europeans and of European diseases. Some estimate that as much as 98 percent of the Indian population died in the first few centuries of European contact. Based on the number of Indians alive in 1900, some estimate that in 1491 there may have been as many 25 million people in North America.

Scientists known as "high-counters" estimate the American Indian population of North America at more than 40 million people. The lowest estimates claim that there were fewer than 2 million people in North America in 1491. The actual number will never be known for certain, but it is known that people did live in every part of the Americas, from the Arctic to Tierra del Fuego at the tip of South America.

FAMILY ORGANIZATION

Among the Indians of the Northeast, the family was very important. Extended families, consisting of grandparents, aunts, uncles, mothers, fathers, and children, often lived together. Among the Iroquois tribes and some other tribes, families were arranged along matrilineal lines. This means the extended family group was traced through the women in the family. In many Algonquian tribes, the families were patrilineal, or organized along the male's family line. In a matrilineal group, a man would join his wife's family. In a group that followed the patrilineal line, a woman would move in with her husband's family when they were married. Often families could recount their lineage back to the very creation of their people. Although families in most tribes followed either a matrilineal or patrilineal form of organization, most tribal leaders were men. In the matrilineal societies of the Iroquois, however, the opinions of women—especially older women—were greatly valued and considered in making decisions for the tribe. When men hold the positions of authority in a group it is referred to as a patriarchal society. When women hold

Opposite page: All but one of the Indian tribes of the Northeast spoke a language in either the Iroquoian or the Algonquian language family. The Winnebago (Ho-Chunk), who were located in what is now Wisconsin, were the only tribe in the Northeast to speak a language from the Siouan family.

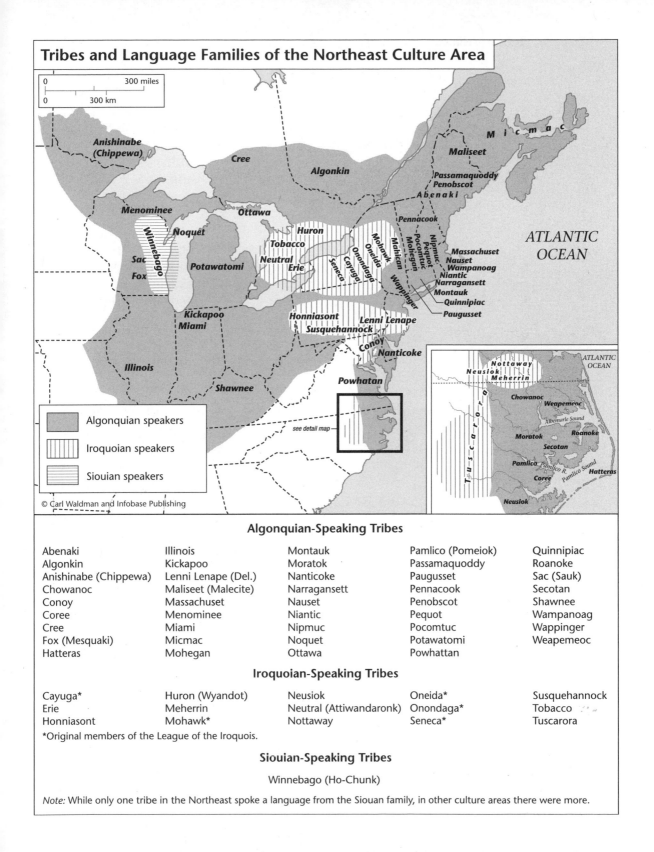

Tribes and Language Families of the Northeast Culture Area

0 — 300 miles
0 — 300 km

Anishinabe (Chippewa)
Cree
Algonkin
Micmac
Maliseet
Passamaquoddy
Penobscot
Abenaki
Menominee
Noquet
Ottawa
Winnebago
Huron
Pennacook
Tobacco
Sac
Fox
Potawatomi
Neutral
Erie
Onondaga
Cayuga
Seneca
Mohawk
Oneida
Mahican
Mohegan
Nipmuc
Pequot
Pocomtuc
Massachuset
Nauset
Wampanoag
Niantic
Narragansett
Montauk
Quinnipiac
Paugusset
Wappinger
Kickapoo
Miami
Honniasont
Susquehannock
Lenni Lenape
Conoy
Nanticoke
Illinois
Powhatan
Shawnee

ATLANTIC OCEAN

see detail map

Nottaway
Neusiok
Meherrin
Tuscarora
Chowanoc
Weapemeoc
Albemarle Sound
Moratok
Roanoke
Secotan
Pamlico
Pamlico R.
Pamlico Sound
Coree
Hatteras
Neusiok
ATLANTIC OCEAN

Algonquian speakers
Iroquoian speakers
Siouan speakers

© Carl Waldman and Infobase Publishing

Algonquian-Speaking Tribes

Abenaki	Illinois	Montauk	Pamlico (Pomeiok)	Quinnipiac
Algonkin	Kickapoo	Moratok	Passamaquoddy	Roanoke
Anishinabe (Chippewa)	Lenni Lenape (Del.)	Nanticoke	Paugusset	Sac (Sauk)
Chowanoc	Maliseet (Malecite)	Narragansett	Pennacook	Secotan
Conoy	Massachuset	Nauset	Penobscot	Shawnee
Coree	Menominee	Niantic	Pequot	Wampanoag
Cree	Miami	Nipmuc	Pocomtuc	Wappinger
Fox (Mesquaki)	Micmac	Noquet	Potawatomi	Weapemeoc
Hatteras	Mohegan	Ottawa	Powhattan	

Iroquoian-Speaking Tribes

Cayuga*	Huron (Wyandot)	Neusiok	Oneida*	Susquehannock
Erie	Meherrin	Neutral (Attiwandaronk)	Onondaga*	Tobacco
Honniasont	Mohawk*	Nottaway	Seneca*	Tuscarora

*Original members of the League of the Iroquois.

Siouan-Speaking Tribes

Winnebago (Ho-Chunk)

Note: While only one tribe in the Northeast spoke a language from the Siouan family, in other culture areas there were more.

the positions of authority in a group it is referred to as a matriarchal society. The organization of families and the organization of tribal structure are not the same thing.

In both matrilineal and patrilineal groups, the life of the family was very similar. The members of the family worked together to supply the needs of the family first. The survival of any family group depended on raising strong and healthy children who would later contribute to the care of the older generations. Childbirth and child rearing were important to the Indians of the Northeast.

When a woman went into labor, she would usually go off to a special house with the older women of the tribe who had knowledge of the birthing process. The survival of infants was not as likely as it is today in the United States and Canada.

CREATION OF THE IROQUOIS

All American Indian groups have a story that tells how they came to exist. Many of the stories share similar elements. Many talk about a world covered by water and the descent of a spirit from the sky world who created the land, plants, and people that inhabit it. The following is a version of the Iroquois story.

Long, long ago the Great Spirit lived with his young wife in the Sky World. In the center of the Sky World stood a sacred tree, and it was uprooted. When the Great Spirit peered into the hole where the tree had stood, he could see a world below that consisted of clouds and water. When his pregnant wife, known as Sky Woman, came to peer into the hole she slipped and fell through. As she fell a flock of geese flew up and caught her.

As there was no land, the geese were at a loss as to where to put Sky Woman. Eventually a large turtle surfaced and offered its back as a place for Sky Woman to stand. Once on the turtle's back, Sky Woman looked around at the endless water and wanted to create a land

In a soapstone carving by Seneca Stan Hill, the turtle from the Iroquois creation story carries the tree of peace and a wampum belt on its shell. (*Marilyn Angel Wynn/Nativestock.com*)

Babies who were born in the winter, especially in the northern parts of the region, had an even lower chance of survival than those born at other times of the year. Those babies who survived were cherished by their families and would often be cared for by many of the older members of the family.

Young babies spent long hours attached to cradleboards, a kind of baby carrier. A cradleboard was usually 12 to 14 inches wide and between two and three feet in length. A baby's father was usually responsible for making the cradleboard, which was often highly decorated with designs and symbols that represented the baby's family and clan. (Tribes are often divided into groups of related families called clans.) At the top of the cradleboard, there was a hoop that served to protect the baby's head

for her unborn child. Animals had come to the turtle to see this new arrival in their world. Sky Woman asked them if there was any soil in their world. They told her that there was mud at the bottom of the water. She asked if they could bring her some.

First a duck dove down but surfaced without having reached the bottom. Then a beaver tried with the same results. Finally a muskrat offered and dove deep. It was gone so long that Sky Woman and the other animals feared that it would not return. But it did, and it brought a small amount of mud with it. With the turtle's permission, Sky Woman put the mud in the center of the turtle's shell and began walking around in a circle in the same direction as the Sun travels. As she walked, the mud expanded into a large area. When she had fallen through the hole in the Sky World, she had grabbed onto a number of roots that she brought down with her. These she planted in the land on the turtle's back, and trees and other plants began to grow.

After the land on the turtle's back had grown into the world known to the Iroquois, Sky Woman gave birth to twin boys. One twin turned out to be good, while the other was evil. The good twin went about creating good things in this new world, while his brother tried to undo them or create bad things, such as poisonous plants. Eventually the two brothers fought, and the good twin won. Because they were the children of the Great Spirit, they could not die. The evil twin was forced to go to a place under the world, where he still lives and sometimes causes problems in the form of earthquakes and volcanoes. Once he had defeated his brother, the good twin created the first of the Iroquois from whom all the Iroquois are descended.

(Author's note: Many versions of American Indian legends, stories, and myths exist. This version was compiled by the authors using a number of different versions.)

Children in cradleboards might be hung from a tree in the shade while their mothers worked in the fields. *(National Archives of Canada)*

Mothers would carry their children with them as they worked. This 1619 engraving was published in a book by Samuel Champlain. *(Library of Congress, Prints and Photographs Division [LC-USZ62-98768])*

and could be used to support a cover to keep away insects or keep out the weather.

When attached to the cradleboard, the baby was bound tightly so that only his or her head could move. This was done in part to protect the child. Dried moss was used as diapers. Babies were taken wherever their mothers went. The cradleboard could easily be carried with a tumpline. This is a strap that went around the mother's forehead and attached to the cradleboard, which was carried on her back. In the house or out in the fields and woods, when the mother was working, the cradleboard was hung nearby so the baby could observe what was going on.

Babies were nursed by their mothers until they were two or three years old. Mothers or other members of the family would often prechew a baby's first solid foods. As the babies grew into young children, they were taught all they needed to know by the older members of their family groups. At an early age, children would begin to help the family with the work that was needed to help the family survive. It was also at a very early age that boys and girls began to learn the separate tasks they would be expected to do as adults. Often an aunt, for a girl, and an uncle, for a boy, would be in charge of a child's education.

Ceremonies were often held within the families to mark important passages in life. From a child's first tooth through puberty, many occasions were marked with celebrations. When a boy first succeeded in killing a small animal for food, it was seen as an important point in his development. However, he was not considered a man until he had killed one of the large animals that were so important to the survival of the tribe, such as a deer or a moose. In some tribes, young men were expected to go off into the woods and live alone for a period of time. If they returned healthy and well fed, they were then considered ready to assume their role as adults. Many tribes also had ceremonies to celebrate a girl's passage into womanhood when she reached puberty.

The spiritual aspects of life were very important to the people of the Northeast. They held numerous ceremonies throughout the year to mark a variety of special events. This 1619 engraving shows Indians in what is now Canada. *(Library of Congress, Prints and Photographs Division [LC-USZ62-98770])*

Once they became adults, the members of the family were expected to marry. The strength of the family was increased by the addition of spouses who could share in the work. Within the family and the tribe, old people were valued and treated with respect for the knowledge they had accumulated during their lives.

Among the early mound builders, people were buried and their graves became part of a growing mound. In later times, Woodland Indians tended to bury their dead in family cemeteries that were near but not too close to the family's main village. People were usually buried with many of their personal possessions. Archaeologists have unearthed pipes, beads, tools, weapons, and other objects from both historic and prehistoric burials in the Northeast.

Woodland Indians often buried their dead in family cemeteries and included a number of the deceased's personal belongings in the grave. This illustration of an Algonquian burial house was done in the 16th century. *(Library of Congress, Prints and Photographs Division [LC-USZ62-569])*

CLANS

Next in importance after the family to many Indians in the Northeast was their clan relationships. A clan is a group of families who share ancestors. The members of a clan believed that their ancestors descended from a particular animal spirit. The clans were named after these animal ancestors. Among the tribes of the Iroquois, there were nine different clans. Depending on the tribe, the clans were named after the bear, beaver, deer, eel, hawk, heron, snipe, turtle, and wolf. Other tribes shared some of these same clan names or had different ones that reflected the animal ancestors in their area. The Penobscot who live in what is now Maine had clans they believed were descended from the bear, rabbit, wildcat, raven, lobster, and others.

When children were born, they became a member of their family's clan. In matrilineal groups, this would be their mother's clan. In a group that followed the patrilineal line, the child would join the father's clan. When a child reached

NATIVE AMERICAN GRAVES PROTECTION AND REPATRIATION ACT OF 1990

Starting in the 19th century and continuing throughout much of the 20th century, archaeologists working in the United States often dug up human remains and sacred Indian artifacts as a regular part of their excavation of a site. The bones and other artifacts they dug up would usually become the property of the university or museum that was sponsoring the dig. Much was learned from these materials, but many Indians and others were offended by the practice of disturbing the graves of their ancestors.

In 1990, the U.S. government passed a law known as the Native American Graves Protection and Repatriation Act. This law gave American Indians control over the burial sites of their ancestors and the power to reclaim the bones and sacred objects that had already been dug. Although this act may hinder some archaeological research, it shows the growing respect for the original residents of North America and a recognition that most people would not want their relatives' remains dug up and used for research.

adulthood and planned to marry, he or she was expected to marry someone who was a member of a clan other than their own. The clan relationship connected family groups to others who were loosely related to them. It also connected them to the spirit world represented by their human and animal ancestors.

American Indians believe that everything in the world is related in some way to the spirit world. That means plants, animals, lakes, rivers, and even rocks are connected to spirits. Clan members have a special relationship with the spirit animal that their clan was named after. Members of the bear clan, for instance, might have a special ceremony directed to the bear spirit. Bear images would have special importance for the clan and might be used to decorate cradleboards or even weapons.

TRIBES

Defining an American Indian tribe is not always easy. For instance, in the Northeast, the tribe known as the Lenni Lenape (originally called the Delaware by Europeans) lived in the Delaware River watershed and the lower Hudson River area in what is now Pennsylvania, Delaware, New Jersey, and New York. They consisted of numerous small bands that spoke two distinct languages of the Algonquian language group. Members of the southernmost bands probably could not completely understand the language spoken by a person from one of the northern bands.

Some also consider the Pennacook to be a tribe. However, they were a relatively small group that lived in one community located near modern-day Concord, New Hampshire. Some sources classify the Pennacook and other small tribes in northern New England as part of the Western and Eastern Abenaki.

As time went on after the arrival of Europeans in the Northeast, tribal distinctions became even more blurred as groups

Indians, such as this Lenni Lenape family, had different levels of commitment to their families, their clans, and their band or tribe. This illustration is from a 1702 history written by Thomas Campanius. *(University of Delaware Library, Newark, Delaware)*

One of the many American Indian tribes forced out of their homelands, the Lenni Lenape lived in longhouses like the ones in this engraving. *(Library of Congress)*

were displaced from their traditional homelands. The best way to think of an American Indian tribe is as a group that usually had common descent, history, language, and territory. The members of a tribe would work together to provide for the common good and defense of the tribe. In modern times, as tribes have been disrupted by interference from governments, it has been difficult for many American Indians from the Northeast to maintain their tribal identity. Using the two examples from above, most of the Lenni Lenape were forced out of their traditional homelands and ended up in southern Ontario, western New York, Wisconsin, Kansas, Idaho, and the Indian territories that are now part of Oklahoma. When most of the Pennacock left New Hampshire, many of them at first joined the Eastern Abenaki in Maine before finally settling in Quebec, Canada.

The political organization of a tribe in the Northeast is also hard to pin down. At times it appeared to Europeans that Indians in the Northeast had strong leaders much like the rulers and officials who dominated life in Europe and in colonial settle-

Metacom (Metacomet), or King Philip, as he was called by the European colonists, was a sachem of the Wampanoag tribe who led a general uprising against the colonists in New England. *(Library of Congress, Prints and Photographs Division [LC-USZ62-96234])*

ments. Metacom (or Metacomet), for example, was the leader, or sachem, of the Wampanoag in southeastern New England. In the 1670s, he led a war against the colonists. He was a respected chief and had followed his brother and father as the sachem of his tribe. Because of this, the colonists gave him the name King Philip (for Philip of Macedon). What they failed to understand was that the warriors who followed Metacoma did so of their own free will. Metcoma had no power to force people to follow him.

The same was true of daily political life in a tribe. A tribe often had a head person, sometimes called a chief or peace chief, who would listen to and suggest solutions to disputes among members of the tribe. But the leader had no authority to force people to accept his or her judgment. Often when a tribe had to make an important decision, a council or meeting would be held and the problem would be discussed until the group as a whole came to an agreement. If a tribe was forced to fight against non-Indians or other Indians, there would often be a separate leader for the fighting. The best warrior of a tribe often was the war leader or war chief. Within a tribe, each village or band might have its own leader who at times would attend councils with the tribe as a whole or with other leaders from nearby.

The size of a tribe affected the social organization of the group as well. Traditional Indian life was built on cooperation to provide for the good of the family, clan, village or band, and tribe. While the smaller units of a tribe might work together in

Many activities of the Indians of the Northeast included religious observances. Successful harvests or hunts, the changing of the seasons, and many other events in their daily lives were connected in some way to the spirit world they perceived around them. *(Library of Congress, Prints and Photographs Division [LC-USZ62-54017])*

the fields and during times of hunting, fishing, and gathering, there were also times when larger groups gathered together. Among the Iroquois, tribes were divided in halves that would compete against each other in their version of the game that is now known as lacrosse.

Other social connections within the tribe would be displayed at times of large celebrations. The Indians of the Northeast had a rich and varied tradition of celebrations that marked the important events in the cycle of the year and in their lives. It is hard to separate the social aspects of the tribes of the Northeast from their religious activities. For most Indians, their lives were closely related to the spirit world that they perceived around them.

Festivals were held throughout the year to acknowledge the spirits who helped the people. For example, an Indian who killed a deer or caught a fish would give thanks to the appropriate spirit. Maple festivals, Green Corn festivals, berry festivals, and others were held as part of the social and religious fabric of the community. There was also a number of religious societies that functioned within a tribe.

One example of such societies were the Iroquois False Face societies. The members of these groups in each of the Iroquois tribes were reported to have abilities to heal the sick, and their members often officiated at important tribal religious festivals. The group got its name from the elaborate wooden masks that the men in the society wore when attempting to cure someone or when impersonating a spirit during a ceremony. Other tribes had similar religious societies.

Members of the Iroquois False Face societies carved wooden masks to wear over their faces. The members of the group were believed to have special healing abilities. They also officiated at a variety of religious observances. This man is shaking a turtle shell rattle, often used in ceremonies. *(Marilyn Angel Wynn/NativeStock.com)*

Many tribes had individuals who were called shamans, or healers. This person was believed to have a special connection to the spirit world. Shamans knew of the healing properties of a wide variety of plants and would prepare medicines for a number of illnesses. American Indians believed the mind and body were closely connected, so it made sense that the same person would treat both spiritual and physical ills.

ALLIANCES AND CONFEDERATIONS

At times, members of different Northeast tribes worked together. In instances such as King Philip's War (1675–76), members of different tribes came together to fight a common enemy. In the Northeast, there were also tribal confederations that existed for a more general purpose. The most famous of these are the Iroquois League of Five (later Six) Nations, the Powhatan Confederacy, and the Abenaki Confederacy.

Shamans were believed to have a special connection to the spirit world. They used that and their special knowledge of plants to cure people.
(Library of Congress, Prints and Photographs Division [LC-USZ62-2182])

Iroquois League

The Iroquois League, or Iroquois Confederacy, originally consisted of the five Iroquoian-speaking tribes that lived in what is now New York State. The five tribes were the Cayuga, Mohawk, Oneida, Onondaga, and Seneca. Later, in 1722, the Tuscarora moved from their original territory in North Carolina and Virginia to New York State and became the sixth tribe in the league.

As the leader of the Powhatan Confederacy, Wahunsonakok (called Powhatan by the English) drew together a number of groups in the area that became Virginia. During his life, peace was maintained between the people he led and the English colonists. *(Library of Congress, Prints and Photographs Division [LC-USZ62-73206])*

No one knows for sure when the league was originally formed. Some scholars point out an Iroquois legend that a total eclipse of the Sun took place when the Seneca became the fifth tribe to join the league. Based on this fact, they have set the date of the beginning of the League of Five Nations to coincide with a total eclipse over central New York that occurred in 1142. This date would make the Iroquois League the oldest continuous democracy in the world. Others argue that it was formed later in reaction to contact with the French in the early 17th century. Still other theories place the formation of the league around 1540.

Whenever the league started, it became one of the most powerful Indian alliances in North America. It kept the five and then six tribes cooperating with one another, allowing the Iroquois to become a formidable opponent to their enemies. For

THE FOUNDING OF THE LEAGUE OF THE IROQUOIS

Iroquois legends state that before the foundation of the league there was often fighting among the five tribes. At some point in the past, a Huron prophet named Deganawida was sent among the tribes to share a message from the Great Spirit that the five tribes should stop fighting one another and cooperate for the good of all Iroquois. He traveled in a white stone canoe. Deganawida had a problem, though: It was very difficult for him to speak in front of groups of people.

Deganawida met Hiawatha, a member of the Mohawk tribe, who was upset about the death of some of his family while fighting the Onondaga led by Atotarhoh. Hiawatha was a gifted speaker. After listening to Deganawida's message from the Great Spirit, the two joined together and traveled throughout the Iroquois lands convincing people to unite with them. Hiawatha and Deganawida are given credit for creating the League of Five Nations. In spreading the word of the league,

Hiawatha is given credit for forgiving Atotarhoh for the murder of his family. Atotarhoh became the first leader of the league.

After hearing Deganawida and Hiawatha's message of peace, Atotarhoh, pictured here smoking a pipe, became the first leader of the Iroquois League. *(Library of Congress, Prints and Photographs Division [LC-USZ62-70238])*

many years, they controlled the fur trade, first with the Dutch and later with the English. To control the fur trade, the Iroquois conducted a number of wars between 1649 and 1654 against tribes throughout the Northeast. These are known as the Beaver Wars, and the Iroquois are believed to have eliminated or nearly wiped out a number of their weaker Indian neighbors.

Eventually the Iroquois also allied themselves with the English in their wars against the French. The French had made allies of many of the Algonquian-speaking tribes in the Northeast and

The value of beaver pelts to the Dutch and other European traders upset the balance that had existed among the tribes of the Northeast prior to the arrival of Europeans. This detail from a 1715 map shows beavers near Niagara Falls. The Iroquois gained more territory in western New York, in part to have greater control of the fur trade. *(Library of Congress)*

The French allied themselves with Algonquian-speaking tribes in the Northeast. This engraving illustrates the 1690 French and Native American attack against Schenectady, New York, in which 62 colonists were killed. *(Library of Congress, Prints and Photographs Division [LC-USZ62-86415])*

sided with these groups against the Iroquois. The strength of the Iroquois League helped protect the English settlements in southern New York.

Powhatan Confederacy

Another Indian confederation was the Powhatan Confederacy. The Powhatan lived in what is now Virginia and had taken the lead in bringing together 32 different bands of Indians who lived in more than 200 villages in the area. When Captain John Smith founded Jamestown in 1607, the leader of the confederacy was Wahunsonakok, whom the English called Powhatan, after his people, as they could not pronounce his name. Wahunsonakok had established control of the area just before the arrival of the English. Much is known about him from the writings of English settlers such as Captain John Smith.

Wahunsonakok's daughter Pocahontas is often credited with saving Smith's life. As the story goes, Smith was captured by the Powhatan, and Pocahontas's father was about to have him

Their *triumph about him*

C: Smith bound to a tree to be shott to death 1607.

Many now believe that Captain John Smith elaborated on the story of his capture by the Powhatan to impress his readers. *(Library of Congress, Prints and Photographs Division [LC-USZ62-31735])*

beheaded when she asked that he be spared. After initial conflict between the Powhatan Confederacy and the English, Wahunsonakok maintained a fragile peace with the English, whom he may have wanted as allies against his Indian enemies. When Wahunsonakok died, his brother Opechancanough became the leader of the Powhatan Confederacy and did not share his

POCAHONTAS
(ca. 1596–1617)

Pocahontas is one of the best-known American Indian women in U.S. history. Her contact with the Jamestown colony was well documented. However, her role as John Smith's savior is questioned by many. Because Smith did not mention her in his first writings about his capture by the Powhatan, some believe he added her role later to make the story more appealing to his readers in Europe. What is known is that Pocahontas was frequently in Jamestown as an emissary for her father, Wahunsonakok, and helped the English settlers in many ways.

In 1613, during a time of fighting between the Powhatan and the English, Pocahontas was captured by Samuel Argall, who had assumed the leadership of Jamestown when Smith went back to England. During the year Pocahontas was held at Jamestown, she learned to speak English and learned many English customs. She is also reported to have converted to Christianity and been baptized into the Anglican Church. At this time, Pocahontas was given the English name Rebecca.

On April 5, 1614, Pocahontas married John Rolfe, one of the colonists at Jamestown. Their marriage helped bring about a period of relative calm between the English and the Powhatan Confederacy. In 1615, Pocahontas and Rolfe had a son named Thomas. When Thomas was two, his parents took him to England. When their ship left England to return to Virginia, Pocahontas became ill. The ship put in at Gravesend, England, and Pocahontas died on March 21, 1617. Rolfe returned to Virginia to tell Wahunsonakok of his daughter's death. Both died shortly thereafter. Thomas Rolfe stayed with relatives in England until 1640, when he returned to Virginia and became one of the colony's most successful tobacco growers.

Pocahontas's story has been told and retold many times, often embellished to make it even more exciting or romantic than it actually was. This mixture of fact and fiction has made her one of the most recognizable American Indian women in the history of the United States.

Ætatis suæ 21 A°.1616.

Pocahontas is often credited with saving the life of Captain John Smith, an English colonist in Virginia. Whether this is true is not known. However, she did play an important role in the survival of Jamestown as her father's emissary to the struggling colony. She later traveled to England where her portrait was done in 1616. This engraving is based on that original painting. *(Library of Congress, Prints and Photographs Division [LC-D416-18753])*

brother's desire for peace with the English. By this time, the number of English settlers had greatly increased, and they had taken much of the land that had once belonged to the Powhatan. Opechancanough hoped to get back his people's land and force the English settlers to leave Virginia.

Opechancanough led two wars against the English, in 1622 and 1644. He was said to have been more than 100 years old when he was finally captured and shot by a guard in 1646 in Jamestown. The death of Opechancanough effectively brought an end to the Powhatan Confederacy as the English colonists in Virginia systematically wiped out most of the Indians in the area.

Abenaki Confederacy

The Abenaki Confederacy suffered a similar fate to that of the Powhatan Confederacy. When Europeans first arrived in what is now northern New England, the Algonquian-speaking tribes of the area were divided into the Eastern and Western Abenaki. The two groups combined into a confederacy, however, as conflicts with English settlers in the 17th century grew and the French in Canada worked with the Abenaki to fight the English. Many of the bands from New Hampshire and Vermont ended up living at Norridgewock on the Kennebec River in what is now Maine. There, many were converted to Catholicism by a French priest, Father Sébastien Rasle (also spelled Râle or Rasles), who supplied them with weapons and ammunition and encouraged them to attack the English.

In 1724, a colonial English force attacked Norridgewock, killing many of the Indians and Father Rasle. Those Abenaki who survived the attack ended up living at two Indian communities, St. Francis and Becanour, in present-day Quebec, Canada.

TRADE

Precontact Trade

In the period before Europeans came to North America, the Indians of the Northeast traded extensively within their region and beyond. Trade items from the Southeast, Gulf Coast, and the Rocky Mountains all found their way to the Northeast. However, many archaeologists believe that most traders traveled within a 200-mile radius of their home villages, with some exceptions. The Ottawa, whose home territory was along the Ottawa River

Published in an 1866 book, this lithograph depicts Father Sébastien Rasle's death in 1724 when the English attacked the Abenaki and the French at Norridgewock on the Kennebec River in what is now Maine. *(National Archives of Canada)*

in what is now Ontario, Canada, are known to have traded far to the west. Like many Indian traders, the Ottawa used the rivers and lakes as their trade routes. From their home territory, they could travel by canoe throughout the Great Lakes.

The rivers of the Northeast were regular trade routes. Many of the rivers and lakes were connected by portages. The word *portage* comes from the French *porter,* which means "to carry." It was used to describe the trails between navigable waterways over which Indians carried their canoes and goods. One major north-south trade route was from the Chesapeake Bay up the Susquehanna River and its tributaries. There is archaeological evidence that indicates that the Susquehanna had been used for trade since around 500 B.C.

In addition to the trade along the waterways, there was an extensive network of trails throughout the Northeast. When Europeans arrived in the Northeast, they used many of the existing trails. The Iroquois trail in the Mohawk Valley of New York and the Old Connecticut Path that connected what became Albany, New York, and Boston, Massachusetts, are just two examples of Indian trails that became important routes for the European settlers. In addition, many of the roads in the Northeast that are from colonial times were built following existing Indian trails.

By carrying their canoes around waterfalls and between bodies of water (known as a portage, after the French word that means "to carry"), the Indians of the Northeast were able to travel and trade over great distances. *(National Archives of Canada)*

Indians moved a wide variety of goods along this extensive network of trails and waterways. The most common trade goods that have survived at archaeological sites were made from stone and shell. Stone that could be worked into tools and weapons was extremely important to Indians throughout the Americas during the precontact period (the era before local tribes had made their first contact with non-Indians). However, the right kind of stone was not available everywhere and was therefore a valuable trade good for those groups who had workable stone in their territory. Obsidian from as far away as the Rocky Mountains has been found in the Northeast.

Wampum, beads made from shells, were also an extremely important trade item. Most of the coastal tribes of the Northeast were known to make wampum. White beads were made from a variety of shells. However, the rarer and therefore more valuable dark purple beads were made from the quahog clamshell. In addition to wampum made in the Northeast, shell items from the Southeast and Gulf Coast have also been found in the region.

In addition to stone and shell items, a wide variety of other goods were also traded. For instance, the Ottawa traded for tobacco, because they lived too far north to grow it themselves. The Ottawa were known to make elaborate reed mats that used dyed fibers to create geometric designs. They used these mats, along with dried berries, fish, and furs, to trade for items they could not grow or produce themselves, such as paints, pottery, and seashells. Although all the Indians of the Northeast were accomplished hunters and trappers, there were some animals that were only available in certain areas. For instance, the Neutral tribe

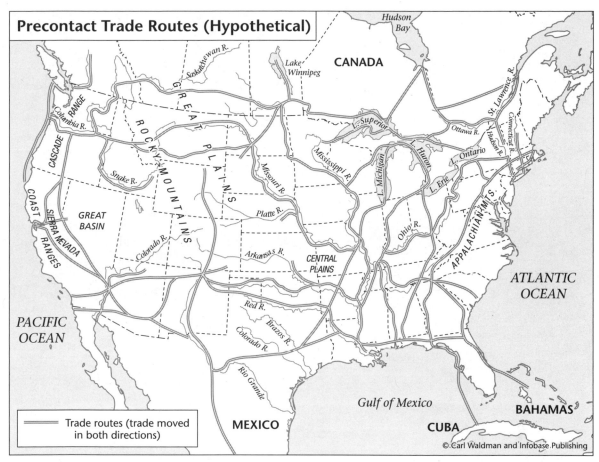

Precontact Trade Routes (Hypothetical)

Trade routes (trade moved in both directions)

© Carl Waldman and Infobase Publishing

American Indians had an extensive network of trade routes that moved specialty goods trade over great distances.

that lived in what is now southwestern Ontario traded black squirrel pelts to the Huron. The Huron would make cloaks from the black squirrel pelts and then trade the cloaks to the Algonquian-speaking tribes to their south and east. Much of the trade that took place in the precontact period was in hard-to-find and luxury items. There was, however, also trade in corn, fish, and practical items such as fishing nets.

To conduct this extensive trade, many traders learned to speak what is called a trade language. This was a specialized language that contained a small vocabulary that allowed people who could not speak the other's language to conduct the business of trade.

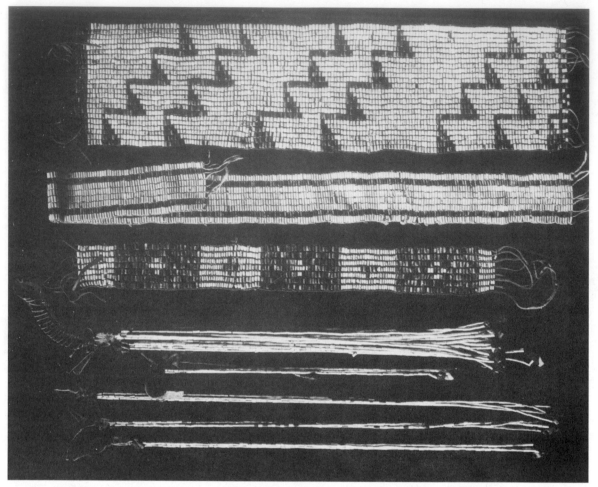

Wampum, shell beads strung into belts and arranged in patterns, was an important trade item among the Indians of the Northeast. *(National Archives, Still Picture Records, NWDNS-106-IN-18A)*

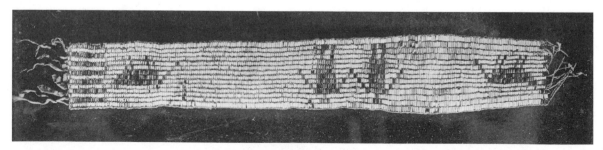

The Wolf Treaty belt shown in this photograph represents a temporary alliance of the Mohawk and the French. The wolves on either end symbolize the "doorkeepers" of the league. *(Library of Congress, Prints and Photographs Division [LC-DIG-ggbain-00161])*

Trade with Europeans

The balance and type of trade that had developed in the Northeast was almost immediately upset by the arrival of Europeans in the Northeast. The French who settled along the Saint Lawrence River and the Dutch on the Hudson and Delaware Rivers established their colonies specifically to make money trading furs. Although many of the English settlers had other motives for establishing their colonies, they, too, traded with the Indians near their colonies for furs.

In the early 17th century, there was a huge demand for fur in Europe. Beaver pelts were highly prized, but a wide variety of other furbearing animals were also included in the fur trade. In addition, deer hides were also in high demand, as the soft leather was a popular material for men's pants in Europe. In exchange for the furs, the Indians of the Northeast received a wide variety of manufactured goods that were unavailable to them prior to the coming of European traders. Glass beads, cloth, iron kettles, iron tools, and a number of other goods were traded for the furs. The items that were most disruptive to the established balance among the Indians of the Northeast were firearms and other metal weapons, and alcohol was perhaps the most disruptive to their societies in general.

The groups, such as the Iroquois tribes that allied with the English and some of the Algonquian tribes that allied with the French quickly, had a military superiority over tribes that had yet to acquire guns. The Iroquois soon controlled all the trade that went down the Hudson River to the Dutch and later the English. Many tribes quickly trapped out their traditional hunting grounds and then moved onto the hunting grounds of their neighbors to try to supply the

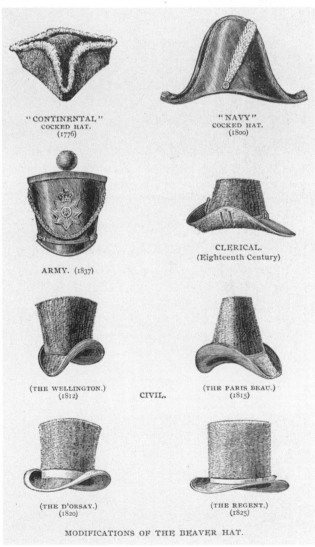

"CONTINENTAL," COCKED HAT. (1776)

"NAVY" COCKED HAT. (1800)

ARMY. (1837)

CLERICAL. (Eighteenth Century)

(THE WELLINGTON.) (1812)

CIVIL.

(THE PARIS BEAU.) (1815)

(THE D'ORSAY.) (1820)

(THE REGENT.) (1825)

MODIFICATIONS OF THE BEAVER HAT.

Hats made from beaver fur were expensive and fashionable items in Europe, causing a high demand for beaver pelts in the Northeast. *(National Archives of Canada)*

The Indians of the Northeast (as shown here trading with a group of English soldiers) soon acquired European firearms and other European manufactured goods in exchange for beaver and the pelts of other furbearing animals. *(Courtesy of Franklin D. Roosevelt Library)*

European demand for American furs. The desire for furs is in part responsible for a number of intertribal wars as well as the wars that took place between the French and British and their respective Indian allies.

3

Houses, Clothes, Tools, and Transportation

HOUSING

In their main villages, the Indians of the Northeast lived in two different shaped houses. Both of these houses were constructed in a similar manner. A frame was made using young trees, known as saplings, which could be easily bent. The thicker ends of the saplings were buried in the ground and then bent to form part of an arch. In houses that are called wigwams, the saplings were placed in a circle and were bent to form a dome. The other type of structure is called a longhouse. For a longhouse,

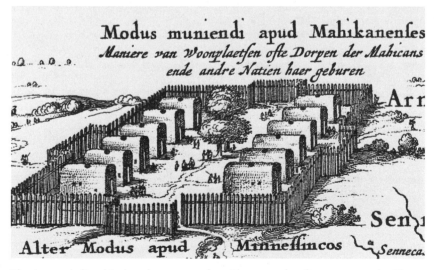

The Iroquois lived in longhouses made with a wooden frame covered with bark. These longhouses are from a detail of a 1685 map. *(Library of Congress)*

45

the saplings are placed in two rows set 12 to 25 feet apart and extending 30 to 200 feet long. The saplings of the longhouse would be tied together to form a long rectangular arch.

In both cases, the sapling frame was covered with overlapping pieces of bark. The bark from a variety of trees was suitable for house building and varied with the species that were available in the different parts of the Northeast. In a longhouse, the peak of the arch was left slightly open to allow smoke out. In a wigwam, a hole was left in the top of the dome for the same reason. During the summer, people cooked outdoors, but during the long winters a cooking fire was kept going inside the house.

The Iroquois referred to themselves as the Haudenosaunee, which means "people of the longhouse." Elm bark was often used to cover an Iroquois longhouse, while the inside was divided up like an apartment house. The average longhouse was approximately 25 feet wide and about 80 feet long. Each apartment was 12 to 25 feet long and would usually have one cooking fire that was shared by two families. Most longhouses might have as many as eight nuclear families (that is, parents and their children) living in them. In most cases, all the families in one longhouse would be part of the same extended family.

Other Iroquoian tribes, such as the Huron, lived in longhouses too. Some Algonquian tribes, the Lenni Lenape, Wappinger,

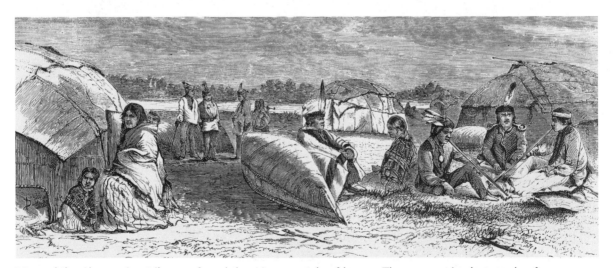

Most of the Algonquian tribes preferred the wigwam style of house. These were circular wooden frames covered with bark. Often the floor was dug down below ground level. This 1871 illustration shows Chippewa birch-bark wigwams. *(Library of Congress, Prints and Photographs Division [LC-USZ62-106105])*

Although wigwams were all built using the same basic technique, they were made in a variety of shapes such as the "domed" and "cone-shaped" wigwams pictured above. *(National Archives and Records Administration, Central Plains Region [NRE-75-COCH[PHO]-623 and NRE-75-RL[PHO]-1072])*

A wall made from logs, known as a palisade, was built around many villages in the Northeast to protect them from raids by warriors from rival tribes. This 1590 illustration shows the village of Pomeiock in what is now Virginia. *(Library of Congress, Prints and Photographs Division [LC-USZ62-54018])*

Mohegan, and others, also built longhouses, but these were often used as communal or ceremonial gathering places. Most of the Algonquian tribes of the Northeast preferred to live in wigwams. In making their wigwams, they would often dig a shallow pit first and then pile the dirt around the base of the wigwam to make them less susceptible to drafts from the cold winter winds.

The inside of both wigwams and longhouses were arranged in a similar fashion. Low platforms were constructed and covered with woven mats as were the walls. During the daytime, people would sit and work on these platforms. At night they would sleep there using furs as bedding. The colder the weather, the more furs were needed to keep the sleepers warm. The warmest furs, which were used in winter, were bearskins. Above the platforms would be shelves and places to hang items. In a longhouse, platforms would run down either side with an aisle in the middle that would allow people to walk through as well as tend their cooking fires. In a wigwam, the platforms would go most of the way around.

Many of the villages in the Northeast were protected by a palisade. This is a wall made by digging a trench approximately three feet deep around the perimeter of the village. As they dug, the dirt was placed on what would be the inside of the wall. Into the dirt pile a continuous row of pointed logs was placed so that they sloped outward with the pointed ends facing the trench. In some of the larger villages as much as 10 acres would be enclosed by a palisade.

At various times during the year, most of the Indians in the Northeast would travel to locations within their territory to fish, hunt, or gather wild foods. At these camps, they would build temporary shelters. A simple lean-to covered with bark was often all they needed to give them a dry place to sleep. In a winter hunting camp where more protection was needed, a small wigwam might be constructed. Where groups traveled to the same places year after year, a more elaborate camp might develop over time.

CLOTHING

Clothing varied little among the Indians in the Northeast, and just about all of their clothing was made from animal skins. The most common skin was from the white-tailed deer and is often referred to as buckskin (a buck is a male deer). The Indians of the Northeast were expert at tanning the hides, creating a soft and durable leather that made for comfortable clothes. Among many groups, the clothing for men and women was very similar. In the warm months, they wore a breechcloth or short skirt that was held up at the waist by a belt.

Some used wampum belts to display their wealth. Others would use a simple leather or even a snakeskin belt. In addition, moccasins were often worn, especially in the woods and

A simple leather breechcloth made of deer hide was the most common item of clothing in the warmer months. This image of a Roanoke chief was engraved by Theodor de Bry based on a painting by John White. *(Library of Congress, Prints and Photographs Division [LC-USZ62-89909])*

Indian footwear consisted of a variety of different styles of moccasins. They were often decorated using porcupine quills and later with glass beads that came from trade with Europeans. *(National Archives of Canada)*

the colder months. Those groups who had moose in their area preferred to make their moccasins out of moose hide. It was thicker, which made it hold its shape and give more protection to the foot. Moccasins were constructed in two basic ways. The difference was in the way the toe was shaped.

In one style, a single seam went around the top of the toe much like a modern hand-sewn loafer. This was known as a beaver-tail toe, as the top piece was shaped much like a beaver's tail. The other style is known as a rabbit nose. In addition to a seam like the beaver-tail style, these moccasins had a vertical seam in the toe as well as a shorter horizontal seam below. When looked at from the front, they look like a rabbit's nose.

Most moccasins had a flap around the ankle that could be tied up around the calf. Usually the moccasins were worn with the flap down. Often the flap and sometimes the toe of the moccasin were decorated. In the warmer months, some Indians went barefoot. In addition, some groups made sandals using cornhusks. In the winter, among the Abenaki and other groups in the northern parts of the region, socks made from rabbit fur were worn in addition to the moccasins for warmth.

Both men and women, especially in the colder months, wore leggings. For women, the leggings were usually only knee high and were held up by straps known as garters. As it got colder, women would wear a longer skirt or a shirtdress that would

QUILL WORK

Much of the clothing and other personal items of the Indians of the Northeast were decorated with porcupine quills. A porcupine quill is hollow, and once the ends are cut off, a string can be thread through to attach the quill to a piece of leather, or cloth after the Europeans arrived. By dyeing the quills a variety of colors, Indian artisans created elaborate designs with the quills. Postcontact quills were often replaced by decorative glass beads and ribbons.

go below the knees for warmth. Men's leggings were longer, covered the thigh, and were attached to the belt. As winter approached, more layers would be added. A mantel or cloak would be worn as an outer layer and was often elaborately made. Special furs, such as black squirrel, and feathers were often used to make a fancier cloak. In the coldest months, a bearskin was the warmest.

In the northernmost parts of the region, people made a variety of fur hats intended to keep their heads warm. The Indians of the Northeast also made a wide variety of decora-

Leggings helped cover and protect men's and women's legs, especially in winter. In this 1890s photograph, an Iroquois chief wears beaded moccasins and a buckskin jacket and leggings. *(National Archives of Canada)*

Headdresses were often made of feathers. This 1935 photograph shows a headdress made of wild turkey feathers. *(National Archives of Canada)*

tive hats and headdresses. These often included feathers, especially those of eagles and turkeys. Headdresses were decorated with quillwork, and beads when they later became available. In addition to decorative headdresses, both men and women were partial to wearing jewelry. In precontact times, jewelry was often made from shells and animal parts, such as teeth and claws. The European fur traders introduced silver jewelry, and it was added to or replaced the more traditional styles of personal decoration.

The fur traders also introduced European-manufactured cloth and blankets to the Indians of the Northeast. At first, cloth was used as a replacement for buckskin in traditional styles of clothing; however, before too long many Indians began wearing European-style clothing, which they often decorated in the traditional style. Today, many Indians have returned to making traditional clothing. It is worn on special occasions, especially for powwows, which are events where Indians from a number of different tribes get together and perform traditional dances and music.

TOOLS AND UTENSILS

Everything the Indians of the Northeast used in their daily lives in the precontact period came from the world around them. They made objects from clay, stone, antlers, bone, and a variety of trees and other plants. Tree bark was one of the most important resources. For the Iroquois, elm bark was used more than any other. For other groups who lived where they were plentiful, the white birch was the principal source of bark.

Boxes, bowls, and other containers were often made from tree bark. These items could be made to hold water by sealing the seams with the pitch from fir, spruce, or other softwood trees. Although the Indians of the region made pots of clay, they could cook soup or stew in their large bark containers by placing hot rocks in the liquid. In addition, the Indians of the region were accomplished basket makers, who used a variety of reeds and grasses to weave. One form of basket that was made from wooden splints split off from a black ash log is still popular today. Baskets were made from many other fibers as well, including sweetgrass, corn stalks, and hemp. Baskets of a wide variety of shapes and sizes were made depending on their use. Everything from backpacks to eel traps were made using basket-making techniques. Some were very plain; others had intricate decorative patterns woven into them. Elaborate baskets woven with a special curled, three-dimensional weave (see photo example in color section) are a specialty of the Iroquois basket makers.

Basket making was an important skill for Northeast Indians as they needed baskets in all aspects of their lives. Baskets of twined fibers were worn on the belt to carry food and other needed items. Large wood-splint baskets were made that were carried like a backpack and could hold a heavy load over a long distance. Other baskets were made with a loose weave to sift cornmeal. Decorative items like belts were also made using basket-making techniques. The materials used and style of baskets varied from tribe to tribe as each group adapted the natural materials that were available to their needs.

A number of useful objects were carved out of wood. Bowls and spoons of a variety of sizes were carved. Those that have survived in museums and elsewhere are beautiful objects that show a high level of craftsmanship. Their functional design gives many of these wooden objects a unique beauty. A large wooden mortar and pestle was also a necessity. These were used to grind corn into flour and cornmeal. The mortar was often made by carving out a bowl-like shape in the end of a large log that had been set upright. The pestle was often large enough to require two hands, as it was used to crush and grind up the corn in the mortar.

Numerous animal parts, in addition to the meat and hide, were used for everyday items. When an animal was killed by a hunter, very little was wasted. Bones were carved into objects such as combs, needles, scrapers, fish hooks, and fishing spear points. Antlers were used as tools for working stone and a variety of other tasks. The sinew, the fibrous material that covers muscles, was used as string. Even the hooves were used to make rattles.

Many people in the Northeast used a wooden pestle and a carved-out log as a mortar to grind corn into flour and cornmeal. This photo is from 1912, but in design the mortar and pestle changed little over the centuries. *(National Archives of Canada)*

Pottery was known to the Indians of the Northeast but was not as highly developed as some of the pottery that was created in other parts of North America. Pottery was made in a number of ways. Sometimes coils of clay were wrapped around a gourd and then smoothed out. The piece was then put in the fire to harden the clay. During the firing process, the gourd was burned away. Pottery was also made by using coils of clay without a gourd form. Most of the pottery of the Northeast was rounded on the bottom. In addition to various sizes of pots, pipes for smoking tobacco were made of clay.

Bowls and tobacco pipes could also be made of stone. A number of important tools that were critical to the existence of Indians in the Northeast were carved from stone. These included hammers and spear and arrow points. Knives, scrapers, and points were made from special stone that could easily be flaked to shape it and create an edge. Stone knives were often attached to wooden handles, while smaller blades and scrapers were shaped so they comfortably fit in the hand without needing a handle.

As soon as Europeans began trading for furs, many traditional Indian tools and utensils were replaced with manufactured goods from Europe. Steel knives, iron kettles, metal axes, and other implements were eagerly sought after by the Indians of the Northeast.

WEAPONS

Weapons fall into two categories that sometimes overlapped. There were weapons that were used in warfare and weapons that were used in hunting and fishing. Fish in the precontact period were extremely plentiful and spawning runs in the spring were common in most of the rivers and streams. At this time, fish could easily be speared from a canoe or from shore. Special three-pronged spear points were carved from bone to use to spear fish.

At other times, Indians used a spear with a stone point to spear large game that was frequently driven into an ambush by other members of the tribe. In the winter when the snow was deep, hunters wearing snowshoes could move faster than a moose or

Snowshoes, made with a wooden frame and leather webbing, allowed hunters in the Northeast to move faster than moose and deer when the snow was deep. This 1619 engraving shows an Indian in what was then New France. *(Library of Congress, Prints and Photographs Division [LC-USZ62-98768])*

The bows used by the Indians of the Northeast were often five to six feet long and shot a three-foot-long arrow very effectively. This 1619 engraving was published in a book by Samuel de Champlain. *(Library of Congress, Prints and Photographs Division [LC-USZ62-98768])*

a deer. In that situation, they would also use a spear to kill the animal and no ambush was necessary.

The bow and arrow is probably the most familiar Indian weapon. Young boys learned early in life to shoot an arrow and practiced on a variety of small game. The bows used in the Northeast are known as long bows. They were between five and six feet long with a string made of three or more strips of sinew twisted together. The arrows they used were more than three feet long and bore feathers to help them fly straight. The size and shape of the point varied according to use. For large animals or human enemies, a heavier arrow would be used. A light arrow with a small point or no stone point at all would be used by boys to hunt small game, such as rabbits and birds. Some of the Indians of the region also used blow guns and darts for small animals.

In conflicts between Indians during the precontact period, three basic weapons were used. The bow and arrow and the

TRADITIONAL WARFARE

War between the Indians of the Northeast during the precontact period was different from the wars that were fought after the coming of Europeans. Precontact fighting was more likely to consist of small raiding parties or groups of hunters who had overlapping territories. For the most part, the American Indians in the Northeast got along with one another. They all had similar technology and enough territory to support them, which removed the motivations for large-scale fighting.

After the fur trade with the Europeans began, that all changed. Different groups fought regularly for the quickly diminishing supply of beaver and other valuable furbearing animals. The introduction of firearms radically changed Indian warfare as well. What had been about physical prowess in often close combat changed into killing each other with the pull of a trigger.

spear were the same as those used in hunting. But the one weapon used exclusively for fighting was the war club. These

were made from extremely dense wood, such as that of the hornbeam tree. The clubs were carved from a length of wood that was about two feet long and had a knot on one end that was carved into a ball. Another type of war club consisted of a similar length of wood, but instead of a ball on the end, an antler was set in the wood with about four inches of the pointed end exposed. Both styles of club were usually elaborately decorated with carving and paint. Being hit full force with either type of war club could often be fatal.

Left: When fighting against other Indians, many warriors in the Northeast traditionally used a war club such as the one pictured here. Tomahawks, small metal axes, were introduced by European traders and were also used in postcontact war. *(Library of Congress, Prints and Photographs Division [LC-USZ62-34156])*

Winter travel was made possible by wearing snowshoes, which kept the wearer on top of deep snow. The Indians of the Northeast also used toboggans to carry goods in the winter. Both are inventions of the Indians of North America. *(National Archives of Canada)*

SNOWSHOES

The Indians of the Northeast made and used snowshoes to walk over deep snow. Without snowshoes, travel in the winter, especially in the northern part of the region, would have been almost impossible. The Northeast Indian snowshoes were not much different than wooden snowshoes that are made today. Although many people now use snowshoes with aluminum frames, traditional wooden snowshoes are still made.

The snowshoes used by Indians in the Northeast consisted of a wooden frame that was about three feet long and 12 to 16 inches wide. A webbing of leather was woven across the frame, and leather straps were attached to the middle of the snowshoe so that it could be tied onto the user's ankle. One modern-day company still making wooden snowshoes is run by the Huron in Canada.

THE BATTLE OF THE SNOWSHOES

During the French and Indian War in spring 1758, a group of colonial soldiers known as Rogers's Rangers attacked a group of Indians in northern New England. Robert Rogers was a New Hampshire woodsman, and he and his rangers had turned out to be a valuable asset for the British as scouts and fighters in the war against the French and their Indian allies. On this occasion, Rogers underestimated the size of the force he attacked and lost the battle. What makes the battle noteworthy was that both sides fought with snowshoes on.

With their snowshoes on, Indians could travel great distances with relative ease in the winter. The snowshoes also made it easier for them to hunt down large animals, such as deer and moose, that had trouble running in deep snow. The Indians in other regions that had snow also used their own design of snowshoes. Exactly when the first snowshoes came into use or which group was responsible for their invention is not known.

CANOES

The Northeast region has an extensive network of rivers and lakes. Using a system of portages, an Indian in the Northeast could travel from Hudson Bay to the mouth of the Mississippi River and beyond. He or she could also travel from Chesapeake Bay up the Susquehanna into the Finger Lakes of New York and then on to the Great Lakes. What is now New England and the Canadian Maritime provinces also had extensive water routes. Canoes of various types became essential for travel throughout the region.

There were two types of canoes made in the Northeast. One was the dugout, which is made by taking a large log and shaping it into a boat. Logs of pine, oak, and chestnut were often used. Once

One type of canoe made by American Indians in the Northeast was the dugout. In this 1590 engraving by Theodor de Bry, American Indians use fire and seashells to hollow out a dugout canoe. *(Library of Congress, Prints and Photographs Division [LC-USZ62-52443])*

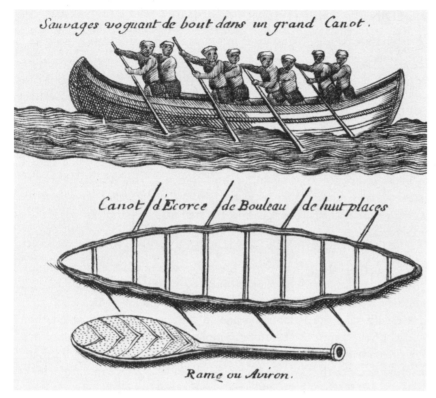

Sauvages voguant de bout dans un grand Canot.

Canot d'Écorce de Bouleau de huit places

Rame ou Aviron.

Canoes made in the Northeast came in a variety of sizes and styles. The large Iroquois canoe pictured here holds eight paddlers. Other canoes were built for a single traveler and were light enough to be carried over the many portages in the Northeast. *(National Archives of Canada)*

the outside was shaped, the boat builder proceeded to dig out the wood in the center to form the inside of the canoe. Fire and stone tools were used to create a dugout canoe. Dugouts worked well and could be easily paddled; however, they were often quite heavy, which made them difficult to carry over a portage. Dugouts tended to be used more in coastal areas, where people did not need to cross land to get from one river system to another.

For the inland Indians, the bark canoe was much more practical. These were made by creating a lightweight wooden frame and then covering it with large sheets of bark. The best canoes were made with birch bark, as it was lighter and stronger than other barks such as the elm, used by the Iroquois. The Iroquois used elm bark because birch did not grow in adequate quantities in their territory. The Iroquois canoes were heavy enough that

BUILDING A BIRCH-BARK CANOE

The first step in making a birch-bark canoe is creating what is known as the inner gunwales. This is the frame that gives the bottom of the canoe its shape. The Native canoe maker would do this by driving a number of stakes into the ground in the shape of a canoe. Inside the stakes, two long strips of wood, usually white cedar, would be bent and then lashed together using the flexible roots of a black spruce tree. Thwarts, or cross pieces, were then lashed into place so that the gunwales would maintain their shape when the stakes were pulled out.

Once the stakes were pulled, this frame was set on a large sheet of birch bark that was bent up around the inner gunwales. As the bark was shaped, the canoe builder often had to cut slits so the bark would take the appropriate shape. As the sides of the canoe were bent up, the stakes were driven back into the ground to hold the bark in place. Once the bark was shaped, the gunwales were lifted up and attached to the top of the bark. A set of outer gunwales was attached to hold the inner gunwales in place and help the canoe hold its shape.

At this point, the canoe was turned upside down on a couple of logs, and the birch bark was trimmed. After trimming, any seams in the bark were sewn together with spruce root. Once the canoe was all sewn up, all the seams were sealed with a mixture of heated spruce gum, animal fat, and charcoal. This would make the canoe watertight. When traveling in a birch-bark canoe, the paddlers would often reseal the seams when they stopped at night to make sure the canoe stayed watertight.

Once the bark was sealed, the canoe would be flipped back over and the inside would be finished. First, thin strips of cedar were run longways inside the canoe. This is called the sheathing. The sheathing was held in place by additional strips of cedar, known as the ribs that went from side to side and were bent into place. To make the cedar easier to bend, it was treated with hot water. Once the inside was completed, the canoe was ready for the water.

All the materials needed to build a birch-bark canoe were available in the forests of the Northeast. Birch-bark canoes were light and durable. This 1871 engraving shows American Indians making birch-bark canoes. *(Library of Congress, Prints and Photographs Division [LC-USZ62-106106])*

the Indians were known to use them as shields during attacks on other tribes. They would even lean them against a village's palisade and use them like ladders to get over the wall.

Bark canoes could be made in a variety of sizes that depended on the intended use. A single hunter would want a small and maneuverable canoe that could be carried easily while portaging from one stream to the next. If the canoe was meant for traveling long distances up the Saint Lawrence and across the Great Lakes, a much larger canoe that could carry a number of paddlers and their trade goods was needed. Today, there has been a revival of birch-bark canoe making; however, most canoes today are made of such modern materials as fiberglass and aluminum. Recreational canoeists across the Northeast have rediscovered many of the Indian routes and portages.

4

Daily Life Throughout the Seasons

SPRING
Maple Sugaring

The coming of spring was most likely greeted with great relief by the Indians of the Northeast. Winters, especially in the northern tier of this region, can be very long and severe. Supplies of food harvested and gathered in the fall would have been greatly depleted by springtime. Throughout the winter, the men of the tribes would have been out hunting to provide fresh meat for their families. As the winter went on, the game close to the villages would become harder to find, and longer and more difficult hunting trips often on snowshoes were required. The coming of spring would mark the tribe's survival for another year. The first important activity of the spring was the gathering of maple sap, which was made into syrup and sugar.

Sometime between mid-February and mid-March, depending on the severity of the winter and a tribe's location, the sap in the sugar maple trees would begin to rise up from the roots. The sap supplies the energy that the tree needs to grow its new leaves for the year. Most trees have an increase in sap production in the spring; however, the sugar maple is the tree with the greatest quantity of sap. The sap of the maple tree also has the highest concentration of sugar (3 percent). The sap run usually begins when there is still snow on the ground. Temperatures during the day need to be above freezing (32 degrees Fahrenheit), while at night, temperatures need to drop back below freezing. The length of the sap run varies from year to year depending on the weather. A return to more winterlike conditions will temporarily stop it. A sudden warm spell that melts all the snow will end the sap run.

For the Indians of the Northeast, maple sugaring was a time of intense work. It was also a time to give thanks to the spirit world. Among the Iroquois and other tribes, a maple festival was held when the sap first ran each year. During this festival, villagers would come together to have a feast, perform ceremonial dances, and offer prayers to the spirits. Prayers were accompanied by the smoking of tobacco. The smoke was believed to help the prayers reach the spirit world above the sky. In the world of the American Indian, everything was linked to the spirit world. Trees and other plants were believed to have spirits, and thanks would be given to them for the bounty they gave to the people.

After the proper ceremonies, the hard work of maple sugaring would begin. Often families would move out of their winter villages to camps in the forest

Collecting the sap of the maple tree was an important activity for many Northeast Indians. *(Library of Congress, Prints and Photographs Division [LC-USZ62-105740])*

where they gathered maple sap. This area, known as a sugar bush, would be used year after year by the same group. A maple tree takes 40 years to grow large enough to be tapped for its sap. It can then be tapped for more than 100 years. The average tree produces between 35 and 50 quarts of sap each year. Forty quarts of sap will produce approximately one quart of maple syrup.

There was some variation among tribes in the way they tapped the maple trees. Some cut a v shape through the bark of the tree and then put a piece of reed or bark at the point of the v for the sap to run out. Others used hollowed out pieces of wood made from cedar or the stem of an elderberry bush to create a tap. During the day, sap would run out the tap and drip into bark containers. During the height of the sap run, each container would have to be emptied numerous times each day. This job often was performed by the women of the group as the men gathered wood for the boiling of the sap.

Before the introduction of iron pots by Europeans, the Indians of the Northeast had two ways of boiling the sap to make syrup. Some groups used clay pots to heat the sap. More common, though, was to boil sap by placing hot rocks from the fire into bark containers. As the water in the sap was boiled off, more sap would be added. Eventually enough water would be boiled off that the container would be full of the rich sweet syrup that is still prized by many—Indian and non-Indian alike. Some tribes are known to have reduced the water content of the sap by allowing it to freeze at night and then removing the coating of ice each morning. After this process was repeated enough times, the remaining liquid in the container would be syrup.

Maple syrup was often sealed into birch-bark containers for use as a sweetener throughout the year. When Europeans first came to the Northeast, they learned how to make maple syrup

American Indians in the Northeast boiled maple sap to make syrup, as shown in this 1724 engraving. *(Library of Congress, Prints and Photographs Division [LC-USZ62-98772])*

MAPLE SUGAR

When boiling down maple sap, if you continue past the syrup stage, granules of sugar begin to form. This process can be encouraged by either rapid cooling or adding something to cause the sap to granulate. Indians are known to have created maple sugar by adding deer tallow to the thickened syrup. They also made maple sugar by pouring the thickened syrup on snow. There is some controversy among historians and anthropologists about the making of maple sugar. Some believe that this practice did not start until European iron pots were available for boiling sap. Others contend that making maple sugar was a longtime practice of the Indians of the Northeast. There is at least one historical source, a letter from Canada in 1684 that was quoted in a London magazine, that asserted, maple sugar making had been "practiced [from] time out of mind."

from the Indians of the region. Maple syrup was so popular with people in Europe that it was described in pamphlets that were published to encourage people to move to the colonies in the Northeast. After Europeans settled in the Northeast, some Indians produced extra syrup to be used for trade. Producing maple syrup is still part of some Northeast Indians' lives.

Fishing

About the time that the sap stopped running, fish would begin swimming upstream into the rivers of the Northeast region. Many tribes along the Atlantic coast and around the Great Lakes returned annually to the same fishing camps. Along the coast, camps were often located at falls or rapids where sea-run fish such as salmon, alewives, shad, eels, and others congregated on their annual trip to their upstream spawning grounds. Many freshwater species in the Great Lakes and smaller lakes throughout the region also made spring spawning runs. Sometimes whole villages or tribes worked together to harvest as many fish as possible at a given site.

During the spring spawning runs, a number of techniques were used to catch fish. One of the most common was the construction of various weirs and fish traps. A weir is an obstacle placed in a waterway that forces fish to swim through a specific opening. Some weirs were made like fences with a latticework of sticks that allowed water through but not fish. Others were constructed of rocks. When the fish came to a weir, they would swim along it until they found an opening and then try to continue their journey upstream. The opening often contained a net that

Spearing fish from a dugout canoe was just one of the many ways that the Indians of the Northeast caught fish. In the background are a number of other methods, including the use of weirs and fish traps. *(Library of Congress, Prints and Photographs Division [LC-USZ62-54016])*

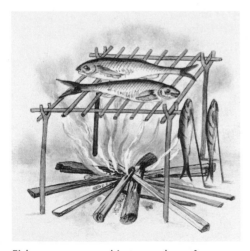

Fish were prepared in a number of ways. In this drawing made by English artist John White in the 1500s, fish are dried or cooked on a rack over a fire. *(Library of Congress, Prints and Photographs Division [LC-USZ62-581])*

trapped the fish. At other times, people would stand near the opening in the weir and spear fish as they passed through. Using either technique, large numbers of fish could be harvested in a short period of time.

The catch would be processed at the fishing camp. After cleaning, the fish would be spread out on racks to dry. In some instances, fires were built under the drying racks, and the fish were smoked. This sped up the drying process and added flavor to the fish. Smoked salmon is still considered a delicacy by many. The large quantities of fish that were caught and dried at the spring fishing camps were divided evenly among the people who had cooperated in the work.

In addition to weirs and fish traps, the Indians of the Northeast used a number of other techniques to catch fish. Many of the tribes that lived along the shores of the Great Lakes used nets to catch fish that swam into the shallow bays of the lake to spawn. At times, Indians in the Northeast fished at night using a torch or lighting a fire to attract fish to the surface where they could be easily speared or caught with a dip net on a pole. In the Chesapeake Bay area, some Indians are known to have used a lasso to rope large sturgeon that would swim into the bay in the spring.

The Indians of the Northeast also fished with hooks and lines. Their hooks were made from bone, antlers, and shells. Sometimes a single line and hook was used. At other times, a long line with numerous hooks hanging from it would be set across a river or bay and left overnight in hopes of catching a number of fish at once.

Although spring was a time of intensive fishing activity, fish and shellfish were caught and eaten throughout the year. Lobsters and other shellfish were included in the diet of the Northeast Indians who lived along the coast. They were also known to have harvested sea mammals, such as seals, where they were available. Some Indians in the Northeast even fished in the winter through holes cut in the ice. Although fish were a plentiful source of food, the most important foods to the Indians of the Northeast were the crops they grew in their fields.

Planting

After the spring spawning runs, the Indians of the Northeast would return to their main villages. At this time of the year, all the people in a village would work to get the year's crops planted. Although individual American Indians did not own private property as Europeans did, in most tribes, each family would have its own fields. Each field would be as big as the family was able to plant and maintain. Corn was the most important crop and was often the first one to be planted, although some tribes were known to plant all their crops at the same time.

The three main crops of the region were corn, beans, and squash. Some tribes referred to them as the three sisters, and their spirits were an important part of the religious observances of the tribe. The three sisters were seen to live in harmony and were planted together in most fields. The corn and beans were planted together in small hills and aided each other. The cornstalks provided support for the bean vines to grow up. The beans are a legume, which means they can take nitrogen from the air and release it in the soil. Corn needs large amounts of nitrogen to grow, and the beans help provide this. The squash were planted in spaces between the hills of corn and beans to fully

SLASH AND BURN

Fire was an important tool for American Indian farmers. Since they had no large domesticated animals such as horses or oxen, the clearing of land for farming took a lot of effort. Brush and small trees that could easily be cut were piled up in the area to be cleared. Larger trees were killed by girdling, removing a strip of bark all the way around the trunk. Once this had been done, the area would be burned to create an opening in the forest that could be used for crops. This technique is referred to as slash and burn.

After a number of years of use, a field would be left unplanted for a period of time. After laying fallow for a couple of years, the land regained fertility, and the field would once again be burned to remove the brush that had grown. When the soil in a field was worn out from repeated plantings, a new area would be burned. If the soil in the area around a village had all been used up, the whole village would move to a new site, where the process of slash and burn would be repeated.

utilize the field. The squash plants grew large leaves that shaded the ground and discouraged weeds from growing.

In addition to the three sisters, a number of other plants were also cultivated. Sunflowers, Jerusalem artichokes, and tobacco were some of the other crops grown. Tobacco had a special place among American Indians and was often grown in special plots that were tended only by the men of the tribe. Tobacco could not be grown in the shorter growing seasons of northern areas of the region and was traded for by those tribes who could not grow their own.

Although spring was a very busy time of the year for the Indians of the Northeast, the survival of the family, village, and tribe was a year-round activity. A poor harvest or an exceptionally severe winter could easily disrupt the delicate balance in the lives of the people of the region. Many of the spring activities were communal in nature, and men and women of the tribe worked together to accomplish what needed to be done. As spring turned to summer, a more strict division of labor between men and women was common.

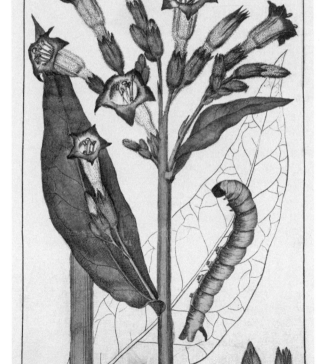

Tobacco was one of many crops planted by American Indians of the Northeast. This is an 18th-century drawing of a tobacco plant. *(National Archives of Canada)*

SUMMER
Farming

For the women and the small children of a village, summer was devoted to tending the fields. Weeding and protecting the crops from animals and insects was a full-time job. The hoes that were used for weeding were made with a wooden shaft and a variety of blades. Moose antlers, deer scapula (shoulder blade), and large shells were all used on the ends of hoes. In addition to weeding, keeping birds and other animals away from the fields required much attention. Often the women and children would sleep in temporary shelters out in the fields so they could protect their crops from nighttime raiders such as raccoons.

One of the most important religious ceremonies of the year came during the

TOBACCO

Tobacco was a sacred plant to American Indians. The plant was used in a number of ways to help in healing. It was believed capable of relieving pain much like aspirin does. It was also used to treat ailments such as asthma, rheumatism, coughs, and other health problems. It was applied to insect bites to lessen the pain and swelling. Most important, it was used as part of religious ceremonies.

Tobacco was smoked during times of prayer as it was thought that the smoke helped carry prayers up to the spirit world. Among some tribes, there was even a special prayer of thanksgiving that was offered to the creator to give thanks for tobacco. Christopher Columbus was given tobacco when he first arrived in the Americas. He took tobacco back to Spain, where smoking it became popular quickly. Tobacco became the major source of wealth for European planters in the colonies of Maryland, Virginia, and North Carolina. Today, people have recognized that nicotine, the primary active ingredient in tobacco, is highly addictive and that smoking tobacco causes serious health problems.

summer and was observed by most of the tribes of the Northeast region. This was known as the Green Corn Ceremony. This ceremony took place each summer when the first of the year's corn became ripe. It usually took place sometime in August. It lasted as long as four days and involved a number of activities.

In this 1590 engraving by Theodor de Bry, American Indians hold a dance at a feast. *(Library of Congress, Prints and Photographs Division [LC-USZ62-40055])*

As the year's crops began to ripen, it was a time to give thanks to the spirit world for helping the people survive. Feasting and dancing were also part of the ceremonies. For the Iroquois and other tribes, it was also when children born since the midwinter celebration received their names. The Green Corn Ceremony marked the point in the year when the community could feel confident that it would have enough food for the next year.

Gathering

As essential as farming was to the Indians of the Northeast, gathering wild nuts, berries, and plants was also an important summer task. The first berries to ripen in the summer were strawberries, in June. Once the first strawberries of the summer were picked, some tribes held a festival. During this celebration, thanks would be given to the spirit of the strawberry and to the spirit world in general for taking care of the needs of the people. Strawberries and strawberry juice would be consumed during this festival, which often lasted from sunup to midday of the same day.

In many parts of the Northeast, raspberries were the next fruit to ripen. As religion was an integral part of life for most of the Indians of the Northeast, ceremonies were often held to give thanks for each food source as it ripened. The raspberry and other festivals during the summer were similar to the strawberry festival. Each food that was gathered also required a certain amount of preparation so it could be stored for later use. The berries that were not eaten fresh were laid out on bark trays to dry. After drying, they would be stored in containers for later use. Dried berries were added to cornbread and sometimes to stews.

Games

Despite all the work that faced people in the Northeast during the summer, they also found time for some recreation. American Indians played a number of games. Boys participated in activities that would help them be better hunters and warriors. They ran races and participated in competitions with their bows and arrows. The most famous game played by the people of the Northeast region was a version of the game that is now known as lacrosse. Among the tribes of the Northeast, lacrosse was usually played by the young men of a village, although there were times when women joined in and other times when women's teams competed. For the tribes of the Iroquois, each village had two divisions, and they often competed against each other in these games. Although each tribe might have a different name for the game in their own language, the game was usually played in the same way.

The Indians of the Northeast created the game that is known as lacrosse today. Among the Iroquois, villages were divided into two teams that competed against each other. This 19th-century photograph shows the members of the 1869 championship lacrosse team of the Mohawk Nation in Quebec, Canada. *(National Archives of Canada)*

Two teams of 15 to 20 players each used sticks with a webbed pocket on the end to throw a ball back and forth between team members. The object was to advance the ball until it crossed the goal of the other team. People who have watched a modern lacrosse game would most likely recognize the game as it was played prior to the coming of Europeans to the Northeast.

In addition to teams within a village playing each other, games were held between different villages within a tribe and at times against teams from other tribes. It has even been reported that games were played to settle disputes between opposing groups. The French in Canada were the first Europeans to play the game and gave it the name lacrosse. By the end of the 19th century, lacrosse had spread throughout the non-Indian population of North America and was even played in Europe and Australia. Lacrosse has gained in popularity and is played by numerous high school and college teams throughout the United States and Canada.

FALL

As summer gave way to fall, the Indians of the Northeast began their preparations for winter. Harvesting and storing the crops from the fields was the first task of fall. It was followed by additional gathering of wild plant foods and communal hunts that often involved the cooperation of an entire tribe. Wood also had to be stockpiled for winter.

Harvest

The harvest of the corn, beans, and squash grown by the Indians of the Northeast required great care to be sure that there was enough food to see the people through the winter. All the members of the community would work during the harvest. Each family would first make sure they had enough food for the winter as well as enough seed to plant in the spring. The seed for the following year was never touched, even if they ran short of food toward the end of winter. If they ate the seeds saved for planting, they would not be able to grow any crops the next year.

After the family had filled its own storage containers, any surplus from their fields would go to members of their extended family who might not have had as successful a harvest. Any additional surplus might be used to trade with other tribes for goods

In fall 1621, the Pilgrims at Plymouth Colony celebrated a harvest feast to give thanks to God and to their Native American neighbors for their help. Many of the Wampanoag were invited to the feast that has come to be known as the first Thanksgiving. *(Library of Congress, Prints and Photographs Division [LC-D416-90423])*

not available within a specific area. It might also be given to the tribe as a whole as a reserve. Because the Indians of the region were such good farmers, they often had enough of a surplus to trade with the early European settlers along the coast. Colonies such as Jamestown, in present-day Virginia, Plymouth, in what is now Massachusetts, and others would not have survived had they not been given, traded for, or stolen corn and other food from nearby Indians. Had the American Indians known what their fate would be at the hands of the Europeans, they might not have been so generous with their surplus food.

Many of the tribes of the region held harvest festivals to celebrate their successful growing season and to give thanks to the spirits for aiding them in their work. It was probably some version of the harvest festival that Indians shared with the Pilgrims at Plymouth that has evolved into the modern American holiday of Thanksgiving.

Gathering

Before, during, and after the harvest, a number of nuts and late berries were gathered. Beechnuts, hickory nuts, acorns, and other nuts were collected wherever they grew and added to the winter stores. In the Great Lakes region, important grain was gathered. In many of the shallow lakes and marshes of the area, a type of grass grows that yields an edible seed. The Europeans misnamed this plant wild rice, and the name has stuck. In the fall, as the seed heads ripened, the Indians of the area would harvest the "wild rice" from their canoes.

Although the plant grows wild, it is known that many tribes worked to encourage the yield of their wild rice crop. Weeding was frequently done and some tribes scattered extra seed into the stands of wild rice. To harvest the seeds, women in canoes would grab a bunch of stalks and bend them down so they were over the boat. They would then take a wooden paddle and hit the seed heads to release the seeds into the boat.

Once enough seed had been gathered, it needed to be processed. The green seeds were first dried in the sun or over a low fire. Once dried, the seeds were lightly cooked or parched to loosen the covering on the seeds. The parched seeds were

Many Northeast Indians gathered wild foods such as acorns and wild rice. This Indian couple is shown eating acorns. *(Library of Congress, Prints and Photographs Division [LC-USZ62-570])*

then placed in bark containers that were lightly hit with wooden poles to further loosen the seed husk. Once the seed husks were loose, the contents of the container would be gently tossed in the air. A breeze would blow the husks away while the heavier seeds would fall back into the container. This process is known as winnowing.

Wild rice made up a substantial part of the diet of some tribes in the Great Lakes area. In modern times, wild rice has become a gourmet item that is quite expensive. Although commercial wild rice production exists, some of the remaining tribes in the area still harvest it using traditional methods. The White Earth Band of the Chippewa, for example, put the proceeds of their wild rice sales into a special fund set up to recover traditional lands.

Aside from edible products from the lakes, rivers, ocean, and forests, people of the region also gathered a number of nonedible items. Hemp was gathered for its fiber, as were a number of grasses and reeds that were used in making baskets. Bark from a variety of trees was also gathered to make everything from containers to boats to houses.

Hunting

Late fall was also a time of hunting for the Indians of the Northeast. The Indians of the region had numerous temporary hunting camps within their territory that they would return to each fall. In October and November, deer concentrated in areas where there were large quantities of nuts or other food. It is also the time of year when deer mate. This time is referred to as the rut, and the male deer (bucks) become less cautious as they compete with each other for the females (does). During the rut, whole tribes often worked together on large hunts. Long fences were built in the woods in the shape of a large v. At the point of the v, there would be a small opening into a pen. A large group of men, women, and children of all ages would form a line and noisily go through the forest toward the fence.

Any deer in the area would try to escape the line of people by running away from it. The fence would funnel them to the pen, where hunters with spears and even knives would be waiting. As deer entered the pen, they would be killed. Once the line had driven deer in the area to the pen, the work of butchering the deer would begin.

American Indians used all parts of the deer. Some of the meat, or venison, as it is called, was eaten fresh, but most of it was dried to be eaten later. Dried venison was added to soups

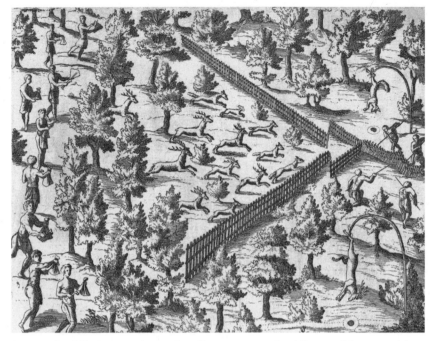

During the fall, the members of a village or an entire tribe would get together for collective deer hunts. Often a V-shaped fence was erected to funnel the driven deer to the hunters waiting to kill them. *(National Archives of Canada)*

and stews during the winter or eaten by itself by Indian travelers. The dried venison was light and easy to carry. It is also very nutritious and that along with some parched corn could sustain travelers on long journeys.

Deerskins were tanned and were the primary material for clothing. Antlers and bones were made into a variety of tools. Sinew, the covering over the deer's muscles, was used as string. Hooves were used to make rattles to accompany the singing and dancing that took place during many religious ceremonies. The meat and other useful deer parts would be divided equally among all those who participated in the hunt.

When not involved in large communal hunts, the men of the region hunted in smaller groups or alone for a wide variety of animals. Black bears were found throughout the Northeast and valued for their thick, warm fur. Moose, elk, and caribou were present in some parts of the region and were hunted wherever they could be found. During the fall migrations, the Indians of the Northeast hunted a variety of waterfowl and other migratory birds, such as the passenger pigeon.

WINTER

During the winter, most of the Indians in the Northeast spent much of the time in their wigwams and longhouses. Cooking fires were moved inside, and surviving the often-harsh weather was everyone's concern. Stews and soups using the dried foods prepared in the fall were the primary meals in the winter.

Winter was when Indians would have time to make new tools, clothes, baskets, and other needed items. It was also when storytellers could practice their art.

SUCCOTASH

The Narragansett who lived in what is now Rhode Island called their stew *msickquatash,* and its main ingredients were corn and beans. To the corn and beans they would add meat or fish, if it was available. Nuts and other gathered foods might also be included. The stew would be cooked by placing hot rocks in a wooden, bark, or soapstone bowl.

The early colonists anglicized the word and called the dish *succotash.* (The European settlers liked it so much, they even named a town—Succotash Point, in Rhode Island—after the dish.) The colonists often added their own vegetables, such as turnips or onions, and salt pork to their version of succotash. Modern cookbooks often refer to succotash as a vegetable dish consisting of corn and lima or green beans.

Storytelling

Although the symbols created on a wampum belt might tell of an event or convey a message, the precontact Indians of North America did not have European-style writing. All of their history, myths, and stories were remembered and passed down orally through the generations. Within each village and tribe, certain individuals were recognized to have a gift in recounting the group's stories. These storytellers were held in high esteem

Wampum belts were most often used to record an event or convey a message. American Indians delivered this particular belt to William Penn in 1682. *(Library of Congress, Prints and Photographs Division [LC-USZ62-86486])*

by the other members of their group. Often the stories that were told involved a mixing of elements. Many of the stories that were later recorded by anthropologists were part history, part mythology, and part lesson.

THE HUNTER AND THE OWL
(A Lenni Lenape Story)

Once a Delaware husband and wife went on a long hunt quite a ways from the village. They had been out several days without having any luck when one night as they were sitting around their campfire an owl hooted from a tree nearby and after hooting laughed. This was considered a good omen, but to make sure of this the hunter took a burning ember and retired a little ways from the camp under the tree where the owl was perched, and laid the ember on the ground, and sitting by it began to sprinkle tobacco on the live coal and talk to the owl. He said, "Mo-hoo-mus [or Grandfather], I have heard you whoop and laugh. I know by this that you see good luck coming to me after these few days of dis-couragement. I know that you are very fond of the fat of the deer and that you can exercise influence over the game if you will. I want you to bring much game in my way, not only deer, but fur-bearing animals, so that I may return home with a bountiful supply of furs as well as much dried meat, and I will promise you that from the largest deer that I kill, I will give you the fat and heart, of which you are very fond. I will hang them in a tree so that you can get them." The owl laughed again and the hunter knew that he would get much game after that.

The next morning he arose early, just before daylight, and started out with his bow and arrow, leaving his wife to take care of the camp. He had not gone far before he killed a very large buck. In his haste to take the deer

back to camp so that he could go out and kill another before it got too late, he forgot his promise to the owl and did not take out the fat and heart and hang it in the tree as he said he would do, but flung the deer across his shoulder and started for camp. The deer was very heavy and he could not carry it all the way to camp without stopping to rest. He had only gone a few steps when he heard the owl hoot. This time it did not laugh as it had the night before.

The owl flew low down, right in front of the man, and said to him: "Is this the way you keep your promise to me? For this falsehood, I will curse you. When you lay down this deer, you will fall dead."

The hunter was quick to reply, "Grandfa-ther, it is true I did not hang the fat up for you where I killed the deer, but I did not intend to keep it from you as you accuse me. I, too, have power and I say to you that when you alight, you too will fall dead. We will see who is the stronger and who first will die."

The owl made a circle or two and began to get very tired, for owls can only fly a short distance. When it came back again, it said, "My good hunter, I will recall my curse and help you all I can, if you will recall yours, and we will be friends after this."

The hunter was glad enough to agree, as he was getting very tired too. So the hunter lay the deer down and took out the fat and the heart and hung them up. When he picked up the deer again it was much lighter and

(continues)

(continued)

he carried it to his camp with perfect ease. His wife was very glad to see him bringing in game. She soon dressed the deer and cut up strips of the best meat and hung them up to dry, and the hunter went out again and soon returned with other game.

In a few days, they had all the furs and dried meat they could both carry to their home, and the hunter learned a lesson on this trip that he never afterwards forgot, that whenever a promise is made it should always be fulfilled.

(Author's Note: This story was copied from http://www. indianlegend.com, which states that "all legends have been edited from historical documents and are believed to be in the public domain.")

For most American Indians, the spirit world and the world they live in are closely interconnected. Their stories often tell of contact with spirits. The plot might include how good behavior is rewarded or bad behavior is punished. By listening to these stories, young people learn what is expected of them as members of their families, clans, and tribes. In addition to stories that remind people how to act, some stories are told purely for entertainment. Each storyteller adds his or her own details to stories. Some stories are similar throughout a tribe. Other stories go beyond tribal distinctions and have common elements repeated throughout the Northeast or even beyond.

Like other Northeast Indians, the Abenaki hunted furbearing animals. This mid-19th-century illustration depicts Abenaki people bundled in many layers of clothing, some of which are fur. *(National Archives of Canada)*

Hunting

Even though fall was a time of intensive hunting for the Indians of the Northeast, winter was also a time when the men spent much of their time hunting. In the northern parts of the region, deep snow forced deer into yards. A deer yard was usually in a cedar or other softwood stand where the deer would congregate. They would browse on the low-lying evergreen boughs. While deer were in their yards, it was easy for hunters to sneak up and kill them.

Moose were also hunted when there was deep snow. A hunter or group of hunters on snowshoes could travel faster than a moose in deep snow. They would track down the moose and kill it. A large moose provided much more meat than did a single deer. Also, moose hide was valued, especially for moccasins, because it is much thicker than deer hide. It is important to remember that American Indians were not hunting for sport but for survival.

Winter was also the best time to trap furbearing animals, as most furbearers have much thicker coats in the winter than they do at other times of the year. Beavers, weasels, mink, otters, rabbits, and other animals were trapped primarily for their fur. The Indians of the Northeast used these furs in a number of ways. Winter beds were covered in furs. Cloaks, hats, gloves, and socks were all made from fur. Furs were also an important trade item between the tribes of the region and beyond. As long as Indians did not harvest more furs than they needed, it remained a renewable resource.

When Europeans began to arrive in the Northeast, they were eager to trade for fur and deerskins, which were in high demand in Europe. The rush to supply the demand for furs and acquire European manufactured goods quickly upset the delicate balance in the populations of furbearing animals. Competition for the quickly disappearing furbearing animals caused numerous conflicts between tribes and between the European countries involved in the trade. The demand for furs continued as the frontier of European settlement spread across the continent.

Furs and the tanned hides of a variety of animals were important to the Indians of the Northeast for clothing and bedding. When they arrived, European traders were anxious to trade for furs. This 16th-century illustration shows an older man in a fur winter garment. *(Library of Congress, Prints and Photographs Division [LC-USZ62-575])*

Midwinter, or New Year, Ceremonies

Throughout history and across cultures, most societies have had ways of marking the end of one year and the beginning of the next. For the Indians of the Northeast, this may have been their most important ceremony of the year. Among the Iroquois tribes, the Midwinter Ceremony lasted as long as nine days and involved a number of observances. Other tribes followed similar observances.

For many tribes, the beginning of the new year was marked by the winter solstice, the shortest day of the year. Other groups timed their new year ceremonies on the cycle of the winter Moon and its position in the sky. Many groups put out all the fires in their village and relit them as a symbol of renewal. Old grievances were supposed to be forgiven and forgotten. Feasts were held, stories were told, and games were played.

Games

If possible, lacrosse matches would be held during the new year observances. In addition, the Indians of the region played a number of other games as well. A variety of dice games were played, and gambling was very popular. The bowl game consisted of dice made from peach pits, which were placed in a wooden bowl. The bowl was banged on the floor, causing the dice to change position, and the players would bet on the outcome.

One of the more popular winter games was known as snowsnake. In this competition, participants slid long wooden "snakes" in a frozen groove in the snow. The winner was the person whose snowsnake went the farthest.

The Coming of
the Europeans

The world of the American Indians at the end of the 15th century was one of diverse cultures that populated the Western Hemisphere from the North Pole to the tip of South America. In the Northeast region, the tribes lived in relative peace. Raiding took place between some tribes, but there is very little evidence to suggest large-scale conflicts between the tribes of the region before the arrival of Europeans. The Indian peoples lived in balance with their environment, growing crops, hunting, fishing, and gathering to fulfill their needs.

Prior to European contact, Indian life was communal in nature with people working together for the survival of their families, villages, and tribes. Land was shared and private property probably only consisted of the tools and weapons that each person possessed. By the time the first permanent European colonies were established in the Northeast, in the early 1600s, the world of the Indians of that area had already been irrevocably changed for the worse.

THE COLUMBIAN EXCHANGE

In 1492, the Italian explorer Christopher Columbus sailed west from Spain in search of a new route to Asia. Instead, he found the islands of the Caribbean. From Columbus's first voyage onward through the period of colonization by a number of European countries and then the expansion of the United States westward, the cultures of the American Indians and the Europeans crashed into each other. In the process, many American plants, animals, ideas, and technologies were appropriated, or

The voyages of Christopher Columbus created interest in the Western Hemisphere among Europeans, who eventually came to North America in such large numbers that they almost destroyed the way of life of the Indians of the Northeast. *(Library of Congress, Prints and Photographs Division [LC-USZ62-59702])*

taken, by the Europeans. At the same time, European livestock, plants, technology, and diseases were introduced into the world of the Indians. This is referred to by historians as the Columbian Exchange. Although much has been recorded about the contributions of the American Indians to the world, in many ways the Columbian Exchange destroyed the pre-Columbian culture of the Northeast.

FIRST CONTACTS IN THE NORTHEAST

Although archaeological proof now exists that Vikings had briefly lived along the Atlantic coast of the Canadian Maritimes somewhere around A.D. 1000, there is no indication that they had any impact on the Indians of the area. However, after Columbus's voyages, John Cabot, an Italian navigator sailing for the English in 1497, explored the Northeast coast from Labrador south to what is now New England. In 1501, the Portuguese explorer Gaspar Côrte-Real made a similar voyage to Newfound-land and Labrador. After these voyages (and possibly before), fishermen from Europe began making annual trips to the rich fishing grounds off the Northeast coast. Fisherman from France, Portugal, and the Basque region of Spain spent the 90 years between Cabot's voyage and the establishment of the first Roa-noke Colony in what is now North Carolina in 1585 visiting the coast of the Northeast region.

These fishermen set up camps on the coast and coastal islands where they would salt and dry fish—often cod—to take back to Europe. It was inevitable that they would come into contact with the Indians of the area. Early in the 16th century, European manufactured goods had already been exchanged. There is evidence that there was enough contact between the European fishermen and the coastal tribes that a crude trade lan-guage evolved that incorporated French and Portuguese terms along with Algonquian words.

As word spread from the fishing grounds of America to the ports of Europe, interest in the Northeast corner of North

The Indians along the Northeast coast dried cod and other fish to be eaten later. European fisherman often employed local Indians at their fishing outposts along the coast of the Canadian Maritime Provinces to dry fish to take back to European markets. *(Library of Congress)*

In this painting, American Indians near present-day Quebec greet Jacques Cartier on his third visit to North America. *(National Archives of Canada)*

America began to grow. Additional trips of exploration took place during the 16th century. The French sent the Florentine navigator Giovanni da Verrazano in 1524, and he sailed along the coast of North America from what is now North Carolina to Nova Scotia. A Frenchman, Jacques Cartier, made three trips to North America between 1534 and 1541. Other European explorers followed, some looking for a route to Asia. Others were hoping to find riches similar to those the Spanish were bringing back from Mexico and Central and South America as they decimated the advanced civilizations of the Aztec and Inca.

Although there were no great stores of gold and silver in the Northeast, the French, the Dutch, and then the English discovered that the abundant furbearing animals of the region were almost as valuable. By the time Verrazano and Cartier arrived in the Northeast, the Indians of the region were already prepared to trade furs for European manufactured goods. The trade in fur between the Indians of the Northeast and the Europeans forever upset the balance that existed between the Indians and their environment.

THE FUR TRADE

The original purpose of New France, as the French colonial settlement along the St. Lawrence River and in what are today the Canadian Maritime Provinces was called, was to trade for furs. Even before the establishment of Quebec and Montreal early in the 17th century, the demands of the fur trade had already reached far inland to the Huron. Before they had ever seen a non-Indian, the Huron were trading furs for European goods. Algonquian-speaking tribes to their east served as the intermediaries in a trade network that would soon extend throughout much of the Northeast region.

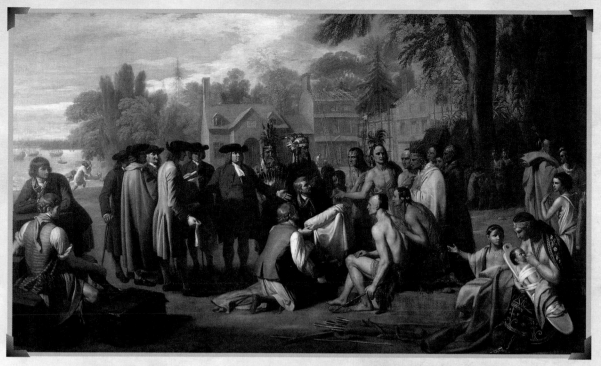

Penn's Treaty with Indians, a 1771–72 painting by Benjamin West that shows the Lenni Lenape signing a treaty with William Penn

Lenni Lenape chief Lappawinze, who signed a treaty in 1737 with Thomas Penn, William Penn's son

Markomete (Bear's Oil), part of an 1831 Menominee delegation to Washington, D.C.

Red Jacket, Seneca leader,
during the Revolutionary War

Seneca chief Cornplanter
in a 1796 painting by F. Bartoli

Sac and Fox leader Black Hawk

Shawnee spiritual leader Tenskwatawa, brother of
Tecumseh, in an 1830 painting by George Catlin

Sac and Fox leader Keokuk, rival of Black Hawk

Wife of Sac and Fox leader Keokuk
in an 1835 painting by George Catlin

Chippewa performing dance to mark the falling of the first snow, in an 1835–37 painting by George Catlin

Iroquois sweetgrass storage basket with lid

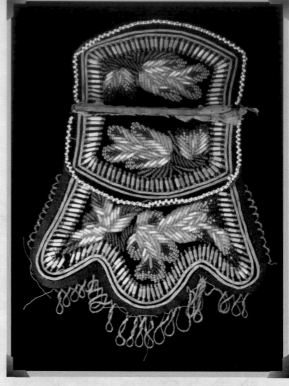

Early 1900s Mohawk velvet purse with colorful tubular and seed beads

Chippewa woman holding her child in a cradleboard on her lap in an 1835 painting by George Catlin

Oneida porcupine quill basket with lid

Two corn husk dolls wearing buckskin outfits, made by contemporary Iroquois

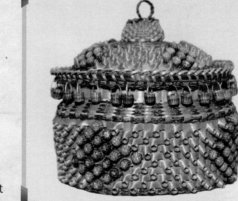

Iroquois strawberry basket decorated with miniature baskets

A recreation of an Iroquois village with bark longhouse, wigwams, and a dugout canoe

An Iroquois corn husk mask

Clan animals on a turtle's back by an artist from the Wolf Clan at
Six Nations Reserve, Ontario, Canada, 1996

Soapstone carving of Atotarho, one of the first Iroquois rulers, by
Cayuga artist Cleveland Sandy

Four Onondaga boys rest while playing lacrosse

Onondaga men singing traditional songs while playing cow horn rattles and a water drum at the spring festival at the Iroquois Indian Museum in Howes Cave, New York

KIDNAPPINGS

Many of the early explorers brought American Indians back to Europe. Most of the time, these people were forcibly kidnapped by the Europeans. Gaspar Côrte-Real captured 50 Indians in Newfoundland and took them to Portugal. Those who did not die during the trip were often sold as slaves after they had been displayed at the courts of Europe. One of the most famous kidnap victims was a member of the Patuxet band, which lived in the area that would become Plymouth Colony.

In 1605, Captain George Weymouth sailed along the northeast coast. Weymouth decided that his employers would be interested in seeing what the Indians of the area were like. Weymouth anchored his ship in what would later be called Plymouth Harbor. He gave a small group of Indians "a can of peas and bread, which they carried to shore to eat." When a young Indian boy came back to the ship to return the can, Weymouth sailed away with him. It is believed that this boy was the Indian named Squanto (or Tisquantum).

Squanto was brought to England and lived in the household of Sir Ferdinando Gorges. Gorges was one of the main partners in the Plymouth Company. During his stay with Gorges, Squanto learned to speak English. When Gorges planned a trip of exploration to North America, he hired Squanto to go along with Captain John Smith. Squanto was to be a guide and interpreter for Smith.

After Smith had finished mapping the area of Massachusetts Bay in 1614, he left Squanto on one of the other ships in the expedition. Captain Thomas Hunt was in charge of that ship. Hunt decided he would try to make a profit by capturing some Indians. Hunt tricked 27 Indians

After being brought to England by Captain George Weymouth in 1605, Squanto, a member of the Patuxet tribe, learned English and later served as an interpreter between the Wampanoag and the Puritans at Plymouth Colony. This illustration shows Squanto teaching methods of growing corn. *(National Archives of Canada)*

into coming aboard his ship. He then sailed off to the slave markets of Spain. He hoped to get £20 for each one.

His plan failed when he arrived in Málaga, Spain, and his captives were taken away from him by a group of Catholic friars who wanted to convert the Indians to Catholicism. Squanto was among those taken by the friars. He remained among the Spanish friars until 1618.

(continues)

(continued)

At that point, Squanto joined a British ship that was headed to Newfoundland. When the ship arrived in Newfoundland, it met up with another English ship whose captain, Thomas Dermer, had worked for Gorges and recognized Squanto. Dermer returned Squanto to England. Gorges outfitted another expedition with Dermer as the captain and Squanto as the guide. However, this time, after Squanto had helped negotiate with the Indians in New England he was to be returned to his home.

Dermer and Squanto sailed into the harbor where Squanto's village had been. They found that everyone there had died in 1617 of European disease. Squanto was the only member of the village still alive. Squanto stayed in the area and would later be a valuable interpreter for the Wampanoag and the Puritans at Plymouth.

The French settlers in what would become Canada were primarily interested in the fur trade and worked with the Indians in the area they claimed. *(Library of Congress, Prints and Photographs Division [LC-USZ62-64110])*

Henry Hudson explored the river in present-day New York named for him in 1609 for the Dutch East India Company. This painting shows an American Indian family observing Hudson entering the river's bay. *(Library of Congress, Prints and Photographs Division [LC-USZ62-107822])*

The Dutch were next to get involved from their bases along the Delaware and Hudson Rivers. Even before they set up permanent trading posts, ships from the Netherlands were visiting the Northeast to trade for furs. After the Dutch established Fort Orange near present-day Albany, New York, the Mohawk tribe of the Iroquois League became the main intermediaries in the fur trade with the Dutch. The Dutch supplied the Mohawk and other Iroquois tribes with European firearms as part of the fur trade. The Iroquois were soon using their technological superiority to displace tribes from their traditional hunting grounds as the rush to trap as many beaver, otter, and other furbearing animals was on. In one four-year period, between 1624 and 1628, 31,024 beaver and 3,087 otter pelts along with a variety of other less-valuable pelts were shipped out from the Dutch colony of New Netherland.

Although the skins from many furbearing animals were traded between Europeans and the Indians of the Northeast, the beaver was the animal that was the most sought after. *(National Archives of Canada)*

The Iroquois soon came into conflict with the French to their north, and fighting often broke out between the Iroquois and the French-supported Algonquian-speaking tribes to the north and east. When the English took over

Conflict between the Iroquois and the French began with the 1609 battle at Crown Point against an expedition led by Samuel de Champlain, as depicted in this illustration by the explorer. *(Library of Congress, Prints and Photographs Division [LC-USZ62-108526])*

This 1613 engraving shows an Iroquois fort under attack by another tribe. *(National Archives of Canada)*

New Netherland and renamed it New York in 1664, the Iroquois became allies of the British. They would remain so during the four French and Indian wars between 1689 and 1762. During the American Revolution, many of the Iroquois continued to side with the British against the colonists seeking independence.

The Beaver Wars, as the Iroquois aggression against their Indian neighbors is called, did much to disrupt the traditional lifestyle of the Northeast. Many tribes were forced to move, and others lost large numbers of people in the fighting. Yet, as disruptive as the fur trade was to the Indians of the Northeast, it cannot be compared to the devastation caused by European diseases.

DISEASE

When the ancestors of the American Indians crossed from Asia to North America thousands of years ago, they became isolated from the diseases of the Old World. Because of this isolation, the American Indians had no resistance to common European diseases such as measles, mumps, typhus, and, especially,

As the number of beavers became greatly reduced in parts of the Northeast, groups such as the Iroquois sought out new hunting grounds to the west where beavers were still plentiful and easily found in the ponds they made by damming up streams. *(National Archives of Canada)*

smallpox. Some of the first permanent European settlements in the Northeast region were Jamestown (present-day Virginia) in 1607, Plymouth (Massachusetts) in 1620, Fort Orange in New Netherland (New York State) in 1614, and the French settlement of Quebec in 1607. However, even before many of these settlements were established, disease spread by fishermen and earlier explorers had created epidemics among the American Indians.

Between 1614 and 1619, a smallpox epidemic ravaged the coast of what is now New England. It is impossible to estimate how many people died, but some villages were completely wiped out. When the Puritans arrived at what they would call Plymouth in 1620, they settled on land that had been home to the Patuxet band of the Wampanoag tribe. The Patuxet had been completely wiped out by the epidemic. Other tribes sustained losses that were

The Europeans who came to North America brought with them diseases to which the American Indians had no resistance. One such group was the Pilgrims from England, who landed at Plymouth Rock in present-day Massachusetts in December 1620. *(Library of Congress, Prints and Photographs Division [LC-USZ62-3461])*

European diseases such as smallpox killed many Northeast Indians, including the Wampanoag pictured here. *(North Wind Picture Archives)*

almost as devastating. Many tribes lost more than 90 percent of their members.

Smallpox and other diseases continued to rage through the Indian populations of the Northeast. The Narragansett, who lived in what is now Rhode Island, lost 700 people to smallpox in 1633. According to one account by four Dutch traders who spent the winter of 1633–34 in an Indian village next to the Connecticut River, of the 1,000 Indian people in the village in the fall only 50 survived to the spring. At about the same time, the Mohawk, Huron, Neutral, Petun, Wenro, and other inland tribes may have lost as much as 50 percent of their populations. According to John Smith, one of the English leaders in the early days of Jamestown, Wahunsonakok of the Powhatan said, "I have seen two generations of my people die. Not a man of the two generations is alive now but myself."

The problems created by these huge losses in population had many serious consequences. A number of groups, such as the Patuxet, disappeared. Some tribes became so small they were forced to combine with others to survive. This may have been one of the causes for the growth of Indian confederations such as the Iroquois League and the Powhatan Confederacy. In addition, the more powerful tribes of the region took to raiding their weaker neighbors and stealing women and children. These captives would be adopted by their captors to replace members of the community who had been lost to disease.

So many Indians died in a short period of time from European diseases that the survivors were often forced to give up their elaborate burial rituals like the one depicted here. *(Library of Congress, Prints and Photographs Division [LC-USZ62-98771])*

FIRST SETTLEMENTS AND MISSIONARIES

In many ways, the very nature of Indian society worked against itself when it came into contact with the first European settlements. The English at Jamestown and later at Plymouth were so few in the beginning that they did not seem to present a threat to the Indians they met. The efficient Indian farmers often had surpluses of corn and other food that they were willing to give or trade to the early colonists. Neither Plymouth nor Jamestown would have survived if they had not been helped by Massasoit, the leader of the Wampanoag, and Wahunsonakok, the head of the Powhatan Confederacy, respectively. Some colonists stole food from their Indian neighbors when they were unable to trade for it.

Not only did the Europeans disrupt American Indian society by bringing disease and new technologies, they also brought Christianity. Many of the Catholics and Protestants who came to the Americas were convinced that their way of life and system of beliefs were superior to anyone else's. This general feeling of superiority allowed the early colonists to justify their mistreatment of people who did not believe as they did. Intolerance was prevalent throughout European society.

Jesuit missionaries spread their message throughout the area surrounding Quebec in New France. In this Frederic Remington drawing, American Indians paddle a canoe carrying a Jesuit missionary. *(National Archives of Canada)*

KATERI TEKAKWITHA
(1656–1680)

Kateri Tekakwitha was born in 1656 to an Algonquian-speaking mother and a Mohawk father who together lived in the Mohawk village near present-day Auriesville, New York. When Kateri was four years old a smallpox epidemic devastated the village. Her younger brother and both her parents died, while the disease left Kateri partially blind and her face terribly pockmarked. Kateri moved in with relatives who were opposed to Christianity and especially to Catholic priests. However, when the French defeated the Mohawk in battle in 1667, part of the peace treaty called for the Mohawk to allow three priests live in their village.

Kateri was fascinated by the teaching of the priests. She was baptized in 1676, and the following year she left home, where she was being mistreated for her beliefs. She ended up in Canada in a Mohawk Christian community known as Kahnawake. Once there she took her beliefs to extreme lengths of self-denial and punishment. She soon was allowed to become a nun and devoted her life to her faith. When she died in 1680, many believe that a miracle occurred: The pockmarks on her face disappeared, revealing a woman of great beauty. In 1884, Kateri was nominated for sainthood, the beginning of a very long and complex process. In 1932, her nomination reached the second stage in the process of being recognized as a saint by the Catholic Church. Many American Indians who are Catholics hold Kateri in high esteem, and many belong to organizations that are still promoting her sainthood.

The leaders of the Catholic Church thought it was their responsibility to convert people to Catholicism. In colonies controlled by the Catholic countries of Spain and France, priests accompanied most of the early explorers and were often some of the first to have contact with the American Indians. One of the earliest attempts at establishing a European outpost in the Northeast was a mission established near present-day Fredericksburg, Virginia, in 1570. However, the mission was soon destroyed by a group of Indians whose leader was Don Luis, an Indian from the area who had recently returned from 10 years of captivity among the Spanish in Cuba and Spain.

The French sent numerous missionaries to live among their Indian allies in New France. These missionaries converted many Indians to Catholicism. A number of the priests also actively encouraged their Indian parishioners to participate in fighting against the English colonists to the south of the French colony. Intolerance was not aimed only at non-Christians. Similar feelings were extended between Catholics and Protestants, and even between various Protestant groups.

When the Pilgrims first arrived at what they would call Plymouth Colony, they were helped by Massasoit (second from left) who was the sachem (leader) of the Wampanoag. *(Library of Congress, Prints and Photographs Division [LC-USZ62-95587])*

Some of the most intolerant people of the time were the Puritans, who settled in most of New England. They came to the Northeast to create a society based on their strict religious beliefs, and anyone who did not conform was persecuted. This extended to the Indians of the area, as well as to nonconforming Europeans. A number of Indians in New England converted to Christianity and were referred to by the colonists as "Praying Indians." Special "Praying towns" were set up for some of the Praying Indians in New England. Yet, despite their conversion to Christianity, they were still treated as second-class citizens by the colonists.

Initially, there was a time of cooperation between the Indians of the Northeast and the European colonists. This cooperation continued on the part of the French, who depended on the Indians in their territory to sustain the fur trade. But this was not the case in the Dutch and English colonies.

6

A Time of War

The Indians of the Northeast who had survived the diseases brought by Europeans to North America and then the competition over territory brought on by the demand for furs were soon confronted by a series of wars. Sometimes the wars were started by the colonists. At other times, the Indians attacked first in an attempt to protect their territory and their culture. In addition, four wars were fought between the French and the English in North America in which Indians fought on both sides. No matter who was fighting or who started it, the outcome for the Indians of the Northeast was almost always the same: They continued to lose land and people through the colonial period and after.

The first contact the Iroquois had with the French leader Samuel de Champlain was in a battle. Throughout the colonial period, the Iroquois would choose the English over the French as trading partners and as allies in a number of conflicts. *(National Archives of Canada)*

POWHATAN WARS

For almost 15 years, Wahunsonakok, head of the Powhatan Confedèracy, maintained peaceful relations with the English settlers in Jamestown. His daughter Pocahontas married John

95

Rolfe, a colonist there, and his grandson who grew up in England became one of the most successful planters in the colony. However, when Wahunsonakok died in 1622, his brother, Opechancanough, took over the leadership of the confederacy. Opechancanough wanted to stop the loss of Indian lands but was reluctant to break the peace that his brother had maintained. In early spring 1622, the colonists arrested and executed one of Opechancanough's warriors named Nemata-

C.Smith taketh the King of Pamavnkee prifoner 1608

Non-Indian settlers often took Indian land and food. Early conflicts, which included abductions and even murders, eventually led to a number of wars between the European settlers and the Indians of the Northeast. *(Library of Congress, Prints and Photographs Division [LC-USZ62-37135])*

nou. He had been accused of killing a white trader. Opechan-canough had had enough.

On March 22, 1622, Opechancanough ordered simultane-ous surprise attacks on many of the plantations. It was Good Friday (the Friday before the Christian holiday of Easter), and the colonists were completely unprepared for the attack. By the end of the day, 347 colonists had been killed, and 25 plantations around Jamestown had been burned to the ground. The losses for the colony might have been even greater had not an Indian boy named Chauco warned some of them. Chauco had become a Christian and worked on the plantation of Richard Pace.

It is said that Chauco told Pace of the upcoming attack, and Pace was able to get his family to safety. Then Pace got in his canoe and went two miles down the James River and warned the colonists at Jamestown. Without Chauco's warning to the colonists, Opechancanough might have succeeded in driving the English back into the ocean. What followed instead was almost 10 years of continuous raids on both sides. The colonists were quick to retaliate and often did not care which Indians they attacked.

Raids conducted by colonists were at least as vicious as the Good Friday attack by Opechancanough. The colonists would swoop down on a village, kill as many Indians as they could—including women and children—then burn the village and the crops growing around it. In Virginia, this practice, which today would be called genocide, became routine. An organized and concerted effort was made to kill or drive away as many Indians as possible.

THE END OF THE POWHATAN CONFEDERACY

A number of modern researchers have tried to estimate the population of the 26 tribes of the Powhatan Confederacy and the other Algon-quian-speaking tribes of the Virginia tidewater. The best estimates suggest that there were almost 15,000 Algonquian-speaking Indians in Virginia in 1610. Through warfare and disease, their population fell to under 2,000 by 1670 and fewer than 350 by the end of the 1600s. By that time, the Indians of the tidewater were no longer a factor. The same fate would befall the Iroquoian- and Siouan-speaking tribes in the Piedmont and the mountains of the colony.

Opechancanough led the resistance, but the growing numbers of colonists and their firearms made it a war the Powhatan could not win. Despite a peace treaty in 1632, raids by both sides continued throughout the colonial period. In 1644, Opechancanough made a last desperate attempt to drive out the whites. Five hundred colonists died in the raids of 1644, but by this time there were close to 18,000 non-Indians in the colony. Opechancanough, who was reportedly more than 100 years old by this time, was captured and shot by one of his guards.

THE PEQUOT WAR

In Virginia, it was Indians against colonists. The Pequot War, which involved the Indians of what is now Connecticut and colonists from the Massachusetts Bay, Plymouth, Connecticut, and Saybrook colonies, was much more complicated. There was a lot of competition between the various tribes and even within tribes over control of the fur trade in the area. The smaller tribes along the Connecticut River tended to ally themselves with the colonists, while some of the larger tribes such as the Pequot were more aggressive and appeared to be a threat to their European and Indian neighbors.

In 1631, Sassacus became the sachem of the Pequot. Sassacus wanted to continue to trade with the Dutch, whereas his son-in-law Uncas wanted to ally the tribe with the English. The two often argued during tribal councils, and their followers began to raid the trading partners of the other side. In 1633, Uncas and his people broke off from the Pequot and started a new community near present-day Lyme, Connecticut. They called themselves the Mohegan, which means "wolf" in the Pequot language. Uncas was a member of the wolf clan and chose that name for his new tribe.

Uncas and the Mohegan tried to remain allies of the English, while the Pequot tried to stop English expansion in Connecticut. After suffering the loss of a tribal faction, however, the situation for the Pequot worsened when smallpox epidemics killed many tribal members in the winters of 1633 and 1634. To make matters worse, in 1634, John Stone, a less-than-reputable English trader, was killed by Indians who were either Pequot or from a tribe that was allied with them. Stone had been attempting to capture Indians to sell into slavery when he was killed.

To prevent an all-out war, Sassacus went to Boston to talk to the leaders there. The officials in Boston wanted only one thing from Sassacus: the people who had killed Stone. Sassacus refused and went home angry. The English did not understand, nor were they interested in, the way the Pequot and other Indians dealt with crimes. Whoever killed Stone most likely believed it right to do so, because Stone was trying to capture people to sell as slaves. In the thinking of the Puritans, non-Christian Indians were not entitled to any rights.

In 1636, John Oldham, a Massachusetts trader who had helped establish the English community of Wethersfield, was killed while sailing near Block Island. His death was blamed on the Indians of the island who were allied with the Pequot. A force was quickly raised in Massachusetts and sent to Block Island under the leadership of John Endicott. There they killed 14 Indian men and burned the village and its surrounding fields. They then sailed to the Pequot territory on the mainland where they attacked a Pequot village. This set off what is called the Pequot War.

In retaliation, the Pequot attacked the fort at Saybrook in September 1636 and February 1637. When reinforcements arrived at the fort, the Pequot turned their anger on the community of

John Endicott led a force to Block Island to attack the Pequot in 1636, sparking the Pequot War. *(North Wind Picture Archives)*

First published in a 1638 book, this illustration depicts a colonial army led by Captain John Mason attacking a Pequot village in 1637. *(Library of Congress, Prints and Photographs Division [LC-USZ62-32055])*

Wethersfield. In April 1637, a Pequot war party attacked a number of English settlers working in a field. They killed nine and took two women as prisoners. The Connecticut General Court decided the time for action had come.

The court voted to place Captain John Mason in charge of a force of almost 100 men from the three Connecticut towns of Windsor, Wethersfield, and Hartford. A large group of Indians joined them. These were warriors from the river tribes, the Narragansett in Rhode Island, and about 60 Mohegan. On May 26, 1637, this large force approached the Pequot village near present-day Mystic, Connecticut. At dawn, they attacked the village by setting it on fire and then setting up two rings of fighters around the perimeter of the village. Those who did not die in the fire were killed as they tried to flee. Most of the Pequot warriors were off on a raid, and it is estimated that as many as 700 people died in the village. Most of those who died were women, children, and men too old to fight.

During June 1637, the English force and their Indian allies hunted down the remaining Pequot. The warriors who were not killed in battle were often executed. Many of the women and children who were captured were given as slaves to the Indians fighting with the English or sent to the slave markets of the Caribbean. Those who were not killed or captured left the area.

Sassacus and some of his remaining warriors went west to the lands of the Iroquois. When they entered a Mohawk village in what is now New York State, they were killed before they could even state their case. The Pequot had been enemies of the Mohawk in the past. To show the English colonists that they were not giving any aid to the Pequot, the Mohawk cut off Sassacus's head and sent it to Hartford.

THE PIG WAR

In 1638, Willem Kieft became the governor of the Dutch colony of New Netherland. Prior to Kieft's arrival, there had been some minor conflicts between the Indians and the Dutch settlers. Kieft saw only one solution to the problem: The Indians who had not died from disease should be wiped out by war.

In this woodcut, Governor Willem Kieft and his Dutch colleagues plot to destroy the American Indians living on land the Dutch had claimed as the colony of New Netherland. *(North Wind Picture Archives)*

First, however, Kieft enacted a tax upon the Indians along the lower Hudson in September 1639. He believed that the Indians should share the burden caused by the need to maintain a military defense in the colony. The remaining Algonquian of the area objected to the idea of giving the Dutch tribute that would enable the colonials to attack them with more force.

Undaunted by the absurdity of his tax scheme, Kieft went forward with his persecution of Indians. In May 1640, Indians on Staten Island killed hogs that had wandered into their cornfield and destroyed their recently planted crops. In reaction to

Under Dutch colonial governor Willem Kieft, American Indians throughout the lower Hudson River area, including the Lenni Lenape, Wappinger, and Mohawk, were killed during the conflict known as the Pig War. This woodcut shows New Netherland colonists attacking Mohawk. *(North Wind Picture Archives)*

the killing of colonists' hogs, Kieft declared that any Dutch settlers who lived near Indian fields should either keep an eye on their animals or fence them in so they would not destroy Indian crops. But Kieft also wanted to punish the Indians for killing the hogs, and his second action is hard to believe today.

In retribution, Kieft sent out 50 soldiers and 20 sailors in summer 1640 to teach the Indians of Staten Island and of the area that would be northern New Jersey a lesson. The Dutch force went on a rampage of murder and destruction, burning Indian fields and villages and killing numerous Indians. At one point, the Dutch threw Indian babies into the river and then shot their parents when they tried to save their children.

This period of genocide against the Indians of the lower Hudson River area is known as the Pig War, or Kieft's War. The fighting between Dutch forces and the Indians lasted for more than five years. By the end of it, many colonists had died, and more than 1,000 Indian men, women, and children had been killed. Although there continued to be conflicts between the colonists and Indians along the frontier settlements, the Indians along the lower Hudson no longer posed a threat to the colony.

KING PHILIP'S WAR

Like Wahunsonakok in Virginia, Massasoit, the sachem of the Wampanoag, maintained a fragile peace between his people and the colonists in Plymouth, Massachusetts, and Rhode Island. In 1660, when Massasoit died, his eldest son, Wamsutta, became the leader of the Wampanoag. During the 40 years since the first Pilgrims had arrived at what they called Plymouth, more and more colonists had arrived in New England. At first they negotiated with the tribes for the land they took. But, as the number of Indians was reduced by disease and the number of colonists increased, the English settlers began to take whatever they wanted.

In 1662, the leaders of Plymouth Colony summoned Wamsutta, or Alexander, as the English called him, to Plymouth to discuss the relations between the colony and the Wampanoag. While in Plymouth, Wamsutta became ill and then died before he could get to his village. His brother Metacom took over leadership of the tribe. Metacom, whom the English called King Philip, blamed the leaders of Plymouth for his brother's death.

Under Metacom, tensions rose but conflict did not break out until 1675. In January, rumors of an Indian uprising were

Wamsutta, eldest son of Massasoit and leader of the Wampanoag, was at Plymouth Colony discussing his tribe's relationship with the colonists when he suddenly fell ill and died. *(Library of Congress, Prints and Photographs Division [LC-USZ62-96236])*

An 1857 illustration quite partial to the colonists involved in the incident, this engraving illustrates the colonists' defeat of a Narragansett village in the Great Swamp (in present-day Rhode Island) in December 1675. *(Library of Congress, Prints and Photographs Division [LC-USZ62-97115])*

taken seriously by the colonists when a "Praying Indian" (an Indian who had converted to Christianity) named John Sassamon reported to the governor of Plymouth Colony, Josiah Winslow, that Metacom was preparing for war. Sassamon was murdered soon thereafter. Metacom denied having any part in the murder. Three Indians were nonetheless captured, charged with the crime, and executed. Throughout the remainder of winter 1675, Wampanoag, Pocumtuc, and Nipmuc warriors attacked small settlements throughout the colonies. The outlying settlements, especially those in western Massachusetts in the Connecticut River valley, felt the brunt of the early stages of the war.

In the meantime, the colonies of Plymouth and Massachusetts had forced the Narragansett to sign a treaty in which they agreed to turn over all Wampanoag who might seek refuge with the Narragansett. In December 1675, Governor Winslow led a large force into Narragansett territory to make sure they were not harboring any Wampanoag. Without negotiation or proof that the Narragansett had violated the treaty, Winslow's forces began burning Narragansett villages. On December 19, Winslow reached the Narragansett's main village, which sat on high ground in the middle of the Great Swamp, which is near the current town of West Kingston, Rhode Island.

Hadley, Massachusetts, was one of the settlements attacked during King Philip's War. In this illustration, Hadley residents rally to fight the nearby Algonquian nations. *(Library of Congress, Prints and Photographs Division [LC-USZ62-75122])*

Normally, this village was a well-defended spot with water all around it. However, the winter of 1675–76 was unusually cold, and by December the swamp had already frozen over, allowing the colonists' forces to reach the village. It has been estimated that 500 Narragansett warriors and an equal number of women and children were killed by colonists on that day. There was no evidence then or now that the Narragansett were ever allied with Metacom.

The guerrilla warfare of the Indians was countered by large forces of colonists and their Praying Indian allies who killed

Sudbury, Massachusetts, shown in an 1857 illustration, was another settlement involved in King Philip's War. *(Library of Congress, Prints and Photographs Division [LC-USZ62-77028])*

any Indians they could find. It soon became obvious that King Philip's War would mark the end of the Indians' holding on to any power in New England. Metacom was betrayed, and the colonists and their Indians allies trapped him in a swamp near New Hope, Rhode Island, on August 12, 1676. When Metacom's body was finally found among the fallen, the colonial commander Captain Benjamin Church ordered that Metacom be decapitated and quartered. The head was sent to Plymouth, where it was put on public display.

In the end, more than 5,000 Indians and more than 2,500 colonists died during King Philip's War. Many captured Indians were transported to the Caribbean and sold as slaves. It has been estimated that the number of dead represented 40 percent of the Indians and 5 percent of the whites in New England at the time. If that is the case, then King Philip's War was the bloodiest ever fought in North America.

THE TUSCARORA WAR

In the early years of the 1700s, settlers in Virginia and North Carolina began to move inland, away from the original settlements along the coast. As the frontier shifted farther west, European colonists encroached on the territory of the Iroquoian-speaking Tuscarora tribe. Eventually, the Tuscarora felt they had to stop the colonists from taking their territory. On September 22, 1711, 500 Tuscarora and their allies attacked outlying farms all along the frontier in North Carolina. In those first dawn raids, more than 140 colonists were killed and another 25 were taken prisoner. The settlers in North Carolina were unable to mount much of an organized defense as each family was trying to protect its own home from attack.

Help came from South Carolina, where a small force of colonials recruited 500 members of the Yamasee tribe and marched north to take on the Tuscarora. The initial South Carolina campaign killed many Tuscarora and burned a number of towns. In spring 1712, Colonel John Barnwell, the leader of the South Carolina force, made peace with the Tuscarora and convinced them to move westward away from the European settlements. The peace treaty might have held were it not for the Yamasee. The Yamasee were not interested in peace with the Tuscarora, captured a group of Indians who were allies of the Tuscarora, and took them off to be sold as slaves. As the Yamasee and the settlers were allies, the peace treaty was broken, and the Tuscarora resumed their attacks on the whites of North Carolina.

This time when North Carolina asked for help, South Carolina sent a force of colonists and 1,000 Indians. A force of 200 North Carolinians joined them. Colonel James Moore of South Carolina was put in charge. In March 1713, a bloody battle was fought near present-day Snow Hill, North Carolina. During the battle, more than 1,000 Tuscarora were either killed or captured. On the other side, the colonists lost only 60 fighters. This put an end to the Tuscarora War, and the Tuscarora left North Carolina to join their relatives the Iroquois in what is now western New York. In 1722, the Tuscarora became the sixth tribe of the Iroquois League.

THE FRENCH AND INDIAN WARS

By the end of the 17th century the land along the Atlantic coast had been incorporated into a number of English colonies, and the wars that had been fought in North Carolina, Virginia,

When European wars between the English and French spilled over into North America, tribes in the Northeast often allied themselves with one side or the other and fought in the wars, as shown in this 1688 illustration. *(National Archives of Canada)*

New Netherland, and New England had eliminated most of the Indians tribes along this strip of land and coast. Many of the Indians who had survived these wars moved to the north and west where they either joined other tribes or tried to maintain their tribal identity in a new place. The Lenni Lenape of what is now Pennsylvania, New Jersey, and New York were one such tribe that managed to escape the onslaught of English settlement. They continued to move well into the 19th century. Today, there are groups of Lenni Lenape in Canada and Oklahoma. Numerous other tribes were not able to do this. Many of the smaller Algonquian-speaking tribes of northern New England, for example, instead combined into what is known as the Abenaki. Many of these people fled to New France and fought with the French during the four wars known as the French and Indian wars (1689–1762).

The first three of these wars—known in North America as King William's War (1689–97), Queen Anne's War (1702–13), and King George's War (1744–48)—were primarily fought in Europe. However, in all three of these wars some fighting occurred along the bordering areas between New France and the English colonies in New England and New York. During King William's War, the French and their Indian allies destroyed Schenectady, New York; Salmon Falls, New Hampshire; and Fort Royal in Acadia (present-day Nova Scotia). During the same time, English colonists struck back at French settlements and worked to maintain their alliance with the Iroquois.

In Queen Anne's War, a large number of the displaced Abenaki from across northern New England ended up at the French mission led by Father Sébastien Rasle near present-day Norridgewock, Maine. Father Rasle had been instructed by the authorities in New France to encourage the Indians at his mission to attack the English settlers. Rasle provided guns and ammunition along with his spiritual guidance, which included preaching that the English were the enemy. From Norridgewock, raids were launched against English settlements in Maine, which was part of Massachusetts at the time, and New Hampshire.

The English colonists tried a number of times to put an end to Father Rasle and his followers. In 1705 and 1721 raiders burned the church and many of the surrounding buildings, but

Hendrick was one of the Mohawk chiefs who helped the British during the French and Indian wars. In 1755, he was instrumental in the defeat of French forces at Lake George in New York. *(Library of Congress, Prints and Photographs Division [LC-USZ62-14987])*

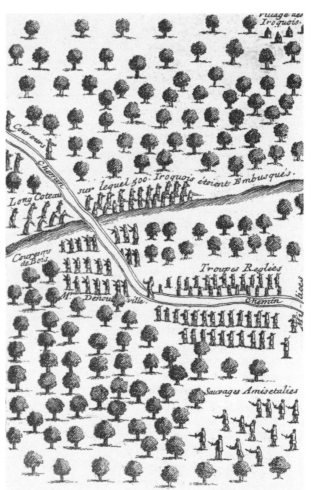

The British and the Iroquois were allies during the French and Indian wars. This 1715 engraving shows the Iroquois preparing to do battle. *(National Archives of Canada)*

During the French and Indian War, French general Louis-Joseph de Montcalm captured Fort William Henry from the British. As the British soldiers retreated, Montcalm tried to prevent pro-French Indians from attacking the soldiers, as depicted here. *(Library of Congress, Prints and Photographs Division [LC-USZ62-120704])*

the English were unable to catch Father Rasle. Then, in 1724, a force of 200 Englishmen came up the Kennebec River in 17 whale boats and caught Rasle. When the leader of the attack, Lieutenant Richard Jacques, asked Rasle to surrender, the priest refused. Jacques then shot him in the head. Eighty of Rasle's followers were killed and scalped, including women and children. Officials in the English colonies had placed a bounty on Indian scalps.

In the fourth and final war, called the French and Indian War (1754–63), North America became the major battleground as the two European powers fought for control of the continent. At first, it looked like the French and their Indian allies were going to win.

In this woodcut printed in 1768, an Abenaki sachem is shown preventing his warriors from killing a captive English officer. *(Library of Congress, Prints and Photographs Division [LC-USZ62-45552])*

However, leaders in London decided to commit the resources needed to defeat the French in North America. In the process of capturing New France, numerous Indian towns were destroyed, and many of the people living in them were killed.

One attack was noteworthy, as it was conducted by Rogers's Rangers, a colonial force of woodsmen led by Robert Rogers. In 1759, as the British prepared to attack Quebec, Rogers's Rangers were given a special mission. The town of Saint Francis was home to a large number of Christian Indians. It was also the base for many of the raids that were conducted against the frontiers of northern New England and New York. Rogers and 200 of his rangers were sent to destroy the town.

Just before dawn on October 2, 1759, the rangers attacked. The people of the town never stood a chance and were wiped out. It is reported that Rogers's Rangers found more than 600 English scalps hanging in the village. The people of New England were much more excited by the destruction of Saint Francis than they were by the capture of Quebec the same day. At the end of the French and Indian War, the British controlled all of North America east of the Mississippi River except for a strip of land along the Gulf Coast known as Northwest Florida.

Robert Rogers led a group that became known as Rogers's Rangers in the fight against the French and their Native American allies in the French and Indian War. *(National Archives of Canada)*

PONTIAC'S REBELLION

In 1762, Pontiac, the war chief of the Ottawa, began to organize the tribes in the area around Fort Detroit. Then they attacked the British on May 9, 1763. With the aid of Neolin, a Lenni Lenape spiritual leader, Pontiac was able to convince many Indians that it was time to rise up against the English and the colonists. The fighting soon spread throughout the Great Lakes area and along the frontiers of Virginia and Pennsylvania. Warriors from the Shawnee, Miami, Potawatomi, Seneca, and Lenni Lenape joined Pontiac and the Ottawa. Fort Detroit and Fort Pitt

As leader of the Ottawa, Pontiac organized attacks on British forts and settlements in the area surrounding Fort Detroit. In an attempt to reach a compromise, he met with Major Henry Gladwyn, commander of the fort. Not pleased with the result of their meetings, Pontiac led an attack on the fort but was ultimately defeated. *(National Archives of Canada)*

were both besieged. Once the British realized the seriousness of the rebellion, they sent forces to both Fort Pitt and Fort Detroit. When Pontiac and his followers learned that the French had signed a peace treaty with the British in 1763, many lost the will to fight. Those Indians who were in the area of Fort Detroit were weakened further by a smallpox epidemic that raged through their camps. In August 1763, Colonel Henry Bouquet with 500 militia defeated a large Native American force at the Battle of Bushy Run, near modern-day Greensburg, Pennsylvania.

By fall 1764, the rebellion was over. During this time, many Indians were killed by war or disease, and many others moved even farther west. After Pontiac's Rebellion, there were only about 1,000 Indians left in all of Pennsylvania.

AMERICAN INDIANS AND THE REVOLUTIONARY WAR

By the time the 13 colonies declared independence from the British Crown, most of the Indians in the settled areas of the colonies had been displaced or so reduced in numbers that they no longer posed any threat to their non-Indian neighbors. The major exceptions to this were the tribes of the Iroquois. When fighting broke out between the British and their American colonies, both sides tried to persuade the Iroquois to fight with them. The Iroquois still controlled almost all of western New York and much of the Ohio River valley.

During the American Revolution, most Iroquois fought with the British against the colonists. In 1778, at Cherry Valley, New York, Mohawk led by Joseph Brant attacked settlers. *(Library of Congress, Prints and Photographs Division [LC-USZ62-111117])*

Joseph Brant was an important Mohawk leader who led his people against the Patriots in the American Revolution. After the war, Brant and many of his followers relocated to Canada, where their descendants continue to live today. *(Library of Congress, Prints and Photographs Division [LC-USZC4-4913])*

Although a few Iroquois tribes, mainly Tuscarora and Oneida, fought with the Patriots, most of those who entered into the conflict fought with the British. The Iroquois by and large saw the British in Canada as their only hope of keeping the colonials to their south out of their lands. During the war, many Iroquois villages were destroyed by the Patriots. At the end of the war, many Iroquois who had sided with the British relocated to Canada, where they thought it would be safer to live. One of the Iroquois leaders of the time was Mohawk Joseph Brant. Brant had attended a school for Indians in Lebanon, Connecticut, where he was converted to Christianity and learned to speak English. During the Revolution, Brant fought with the British. After they were defeated, he led a group of Mohawk to settle in Ontario, Canada. Several places in Ontario, including Brant's Town, Brantford, and Brant County, are named after him. By the end of the Revolution, only the Indians in the unsettled western part of the Northeast could mount a threat to the United States.

7

Indians of the Northeast in the Nineteenth Century

♛ FIGHT FOR THE OLD NORTHWEST

After the Revolution, the newly formed United States turned its attention to what was then called the Northwest Territory. This included the part of the Northeast Culture Area between the Appalachian Mountains and the Mississippi River north to the area around the Great Lakes. Many of the tribes in this area had been killed or forced to move during the Beaver Wars of the 17th century. During the 18th century, groups from east of the mountains, such as the Lenni Lenape, Shawnee, Seneca, and others, relocated into the Ohio River watershed as they were forced out of their traditional homelands by European settlers.

Warriors from these tribes had joined in Pontiac's Rebellion and sided with the British during the American Revolution. President George Washington, in his first year in office, began a long series of attempts by the U.S. government to eliminate or remove the Indians of what is now called the Old Northwest. The pattern started in 1790 with what is called Little Turtle's War. It would continue throughout the 19th century until almost all of the tribes of the Old Northwest had been wiped out or had moved west of the Mississippi River into what was called Indian Territory.

Little Turtle's War

Little Turtle (Michikinikwa) was a leader of the Miami tribe who, beginning in 1790, led a force made up of warriors from his own tribe as well as from the Shawnee, Chippewa, Lenni Lenape, Potawatomi, and Ottawa. For the first year of the conflict, Little Turtle and his followers held their own and then on

115

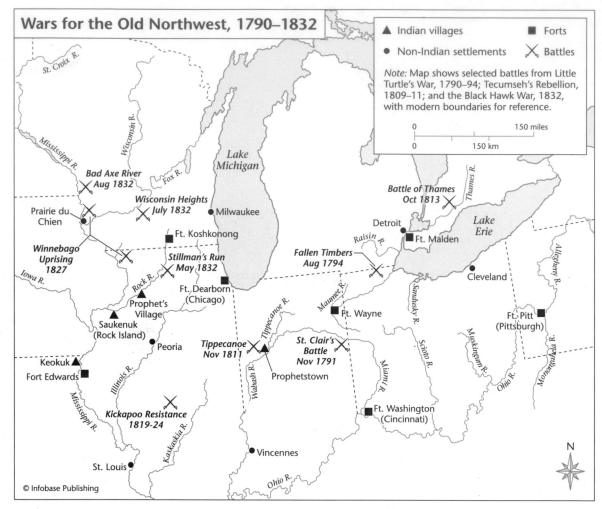

Wars for the Old Northwest, 1790–1832

▲ Indian villages   ■ Forts
● Non-Indian settlements   ✕ Battles

Note: Map shows selected battles from Little Turtle's War, 1790–94; Tecumseh's Rebellion, 1809–11; and the Black Hawk War, 1832, with modern boundaries for reference.

0 ——————— 150 miles
0 ——————— 150 km

St. Croix R.
Wisconsin R.
Mississippi R.
Fox R.
Lake Michigan

Bad Axe River Aug 1832
Wisconsin Heights July 1832
● Milwaukee

Prairie du Chien
Winnebago Uprising 1827
Iowa R.
Ft. Koshkonong
Stillman's Run May 1832
Rock R.
▲ Prophet's Village
Saukenuk (Rock Island)
Ft. Dearborn (Chicago)

Keokuk ▲
Fort Edwards ■
Illinois R.
● Peoria
Kickapoo Resistance 1819-24
Kaskaskia R.
St. Louis ●
Mississippi R.

Tippecanoe Nov 1811
Wabash R.
Tippecanoe R.
▲ Prophetstown
● Vincennes
Ohio R.

St. Clair's Battle Nov 1791
Maumee R.
■ Ft. Wayne
Miami R.
Fallen Timbers Aug 1794
Raisin R.
Detroit
■ Ft. Malden
Lake Erie

Battle of Thames Oct 1813
Thames R.

Sandusky R.
Scioto R.
● Cleveland
Allegheny R.
Ft. Pitt (Pittsburgh) ■
Muskingum R.
Ohio R.
Monongahela R.

■ Ft. Washington (Cincinnati)

N

© Infobase Publishing

The Old Northwest is now the states of Ohio, Michigan, Indiana, Illinois, and Wisconsin and was an area of many conflicts between Indians and white settlers.

November 3, 1791, defeated a large force of soldiers made up of 2,000 recent enlistees under General Arthur St. Clair. After Little Turtle's victory, President Washington sent General Anthony Wayne with 3,000 seasoned troops to take on Little Turtle. By 1794, Wayne had gained the upper hand. On August 20, 1794, at Fallen Timbers near the western end of Lake Erie, Wayne won a decisive victory in which hundreds of Little Turtle's followers were killed, while Wayne lost fewer than 50 men.

Wayne next had his forces burn crops and villages all over the Ohio River area, making winter very hard for these Indians.

Little Turtle, shown in a woodcut, was a leader of the Miami. *(North Wind Picture Archives)*

General Anthony Wayne defeated Little Turtle and his followers at Fallen Timbers, in present-day Ohio, in 1794. *(Library of Congress, Prints and Photographs Division [LC-USZ62-5667])*

By the next year, the Indians of the area had had enough. On August 3, 1795, Little Turtle and more than 1,000 chiefs and warriors signed the Treaty of Greenville in which they gave up all of the land that is present-day Ohio and much of Indiana. The pattern had been set. An Indian leader would try to organize a fighting force from a number of tribes to resist the expansion of the United States into Indian lands. The U.S. government would eventually send enough troops to defeat the Indians and then would take as much of their land as they could.

Tecumseh's Rebellion

Tecumseh was a Shawnee chief who had refused to take part in the Treaty of Greenville in 1795 because he felt the land had been given to the tribes by the creator and could not be sold or given away. Tecumseh understood that no individual group of Indians could resist the U.S. government. His plan, therefore, was to unite all the tribes that lived east of the Mississippi River from the Gulf of Mexico north to Canada. Tecumseh was a forceful speaker who traveled throughout the region speaking of his plan for Indian unity. Many believed in his cause and joined him.

One of Tecumseh's staunchest supporters was his brother Tenskwatawa, who claimed to have received a message from the creator. Tenskwatawa was considered a prophet (he is sometimes called the Shawnee Prophet), and the message he spread was one of returning to traditional Indian ways. This included no drinking of alcohol, which was regularly traded to Indians. Together, Tecumseh and Tenskwatawa established a town where the Tippecanoe and Wabash Rivers come together. Some referred to the town as Tippecanoe; others called it Prophetstown.

During the first decade of the 19th century, Tecumseh continued to travel and speak to Indians throughout the area. In 1809, while Tecumseh was away, William Henry Harrison, who was the governor of Indiana Territory and would later be president of the United States, gathered a group of tribal chiefs. He lied to them, and he supplied them with as much alcohol as

INDIAN RELIGIOUS MOVEMENTS

As a prophet, Tenskwatawa preached a return to Indian ways and helped Tecumseh as he tried to organize the Indians of the Old Northwest. There were a number of other Indian prophets who appeared during these troubled times. Kennekuk was a Kickapoo prophet who called for a rejection of white culture. White Cloud (Wabokisheik), a member of the Winnebago tribe, also preached resistance against white expansion and a return to Indian ways. He was instrumental in the last war in the Old Northwest, known as the Black Hawk War.

Not all Indian prophets of the time preached against the whites. Handsome Lake (Skaniadariio) was a Seneca leader, and half brother of chief Cornplanter, who preached a value system that was in part based on Christian beliefs. He talked about family values and encouraged the Iroquois to send their children to school so they could learn the ways of white society. Handsome Lake had a large following among the Iroquois who hoped to live next to and in harmony with their white neighbors. Other Iroquois objected to these beliefs, and a division was created within the tribes. The teachings of Handsome Lake were written down as the Code of Handsome Lake after his death and are still followed by many Iroquois in what became known as the Longhouse religion.

they wanted. Harrison then got the chiefs to sign away 3 million acres of land that was not really theirs in what is known as the Treaty of Fort Wayne.

Tecumseh was angered by this and confronted the governor, but he felt his alliance was not yet ready to go to war. In 1811, Harrison and Tecumseh were once again on the verge of violent confrontation when the governor demanded that some warriors living at Tippecanoe be turned over to him for having killed settlers in Illinois. Tecumseh did not give up the warriors, who were members of the Potawatomi tribe, but he again avoided open conflict. After this incident, Tecumseh once again traveled to the south to recruit more Indians to his alliance.

While Tecumseh was gone, Harrison returned to Tippecanoe with 1,000 militia. Tecumseh had warned his followers that they were not yet ready for war, but Tenskwatawa had convinced many that his magic would protect them from the bullets of the soldiers. At dawn on November 7, 1811, Tenskwatawa

William Henry Harrison governed Indiana Territory from 1800 until 1812. In 1809, he tricked the Miami, Potawatomi, and Lenni Lenape into signing 3 million acres of land over to the territory. *(Library of Congress, Prints and Photographs Division [LC-USZ62-118276])*

attempted a sneak attack on Harrison's force. Harrison had set up his camp in a defensive circle and posted sentries to warn of any attack. Although more than 60 soldiers were killed and 100 were wounded, they were able to hold off Tenskwatawa's force.

When Harrison moved on Tippecanoe later that day, everyone had fled. His men burned the town and all the supplies that Tecumseh had stockpiled for his war against the United States. Tecumseh's hopes for an organized rebellion ended with the destruction of Tippecanoe, and Tenskwatawa had lost most of his credibility as his magic had failed to stop the soldiers' bullets. Numerous groups began conducting small raids against settlers.

When war broke out between the British and the Americans in 1812, Tecumseh saw one last opportunity. He allied himself with the British in Canada and went to war against the United States. With Tecumseh's help, British troops captured the forts at Detroit and Chicago. The British leader General Isaac Brock was killed in battle, and his replacement soon abandoned his Indian allies. The Americans defeated a large British naval force on Lake Erie, and the British soldiers who had been fighting with Tecumseh returned to Canada.

Tecumseh and his force covered the British retreat. On October 5, 1813, a Kentucky militia force fought Tecumseh at the Battle of the Thames in Ontario. During this battle, Tecumseh was killed. His men are reported to have hidden his body, and the Kentuckians skinned a fallen warrior whom they thought was Tecumseh. Had the British not abandoned him, Tecumseh might have achieved his goal of uniting the Indians of the Old Northwest and stopping the expansion of the United States into Indian lands.

AMERICAN ALLIES IN THE WAR OF 1812

During the War of 1812 between the United States and Great Britain, many Indians, such as Tecumseh, joined the British, hoping that a British victory would halt the westward expansion of the United States. However, not all Indians sided with the British. Seneca leader Red Jacket (Sagoyewatha) had fought with the British during the American Revolution but after the war negotiated the peace between the Iroquois who stayed in New York and the new U.S. government. When war broke out between the United States and Great Britain in 1812, Red Jacket sided with the Americans.

Right: Sagoyewatha, whose English name was Red Jacket, had allied the Seneca with the British during the American Revolution. After the Revolution, he supported the new U.S. government and encouraged his followers to side with the Americans in the War of 1812.
(Library of Congress, Prints and Photographs Division [LC-USZ62-128675])

Tecumseh tried to unify the Indians in the Old Northwest and beyond. Although he was unsuccessful, he was able to help the British capture forts at Detroit and Chicago before being killed at the Battle of the Thames in Ontario near the end of the War of 1812. *(Library of Congress, Prints and Photographs Division [LC-USZ62-10173])*

Kickapoo Resistance

After the defeat of Tecumseh, other tribes continued to resist the westward expansion of white settlement. The Kickapoo, who lived in present-day Illinois between the Illinois and Wabash Rivers, were the next to fight to hold on to their traditional homelands. A band of Kickapoo led by their chief Mecina resisted federal authorities who were trying to get the Kickapoo to give up their land. Mecina, like Tecumseh, did not believe Indian land should be sold, but Mecina did not have enough followers to mount a major campaign against the government. Instead, they attacked settlers who were moving onto Indian lands. When the military defeated Mecina's band, he joined with the Kickapoo prophet Kennekuk in an attempt to keep Kickapoo lands. Kennekuk and Mecina knew they could not win, but they tried to stall the eventual removal of their people from their lands. These tactics worked for a while. However, in 1833, the Kickapoo were relocated to land west of the Mississippi River in what is now Kansas. Some of Mecina's followers wanted to continue to fight and joined Black Hawk in his war against the United States.

Winnebago Uprising

The greed of the U.S. government knew no bounds in its campaign against the Indians of the Old Northwest. The Winnebago (Ho-Chunk) who lived along what is now the border between Illinois and Wisconsin had discovered deposits of lead on their land. In the 1820s, they began mining the lead and selling it to white traders. The government feared that if the Winnebago were successful in their mining operations, they would never willingly give up their lands. Indian agents in the area were instructed to try to stop the Winnebago from developing their mine.

In 1827, an event took place that gave the government the excuse it needed to attack the Winnebago. White traders in two keelboats stopped at a village led by Red Bird. After spending the night drinking with a group of Winnebago, the boatmen kidnapped several Winnebago women and headed downriver. Red Bird led a group of warriors in hope of recovering the kidnapped women.

On June 30, Red Bird and his followers caught up with the boats. In the fight, four whites and 12 Indians were killed; the women were able to escape from the boats. Large numbers of troops from Illinois that included militia volunteers and regular federal troops moved against the Winnebago. Many Winnebago did not want to become part of the fight and negotiated with the military to avoid bloodshed. Once the military had isolated Red Bird and his followers, there was no hope for an Indian victory. Red Bird agreed to surrender in exchange for the lives of his followers. Red Bird died in January 1828 in jail, awaiting his trial.

The Winnebago leaders who had made peace with the military were forced to sign a treaty in August 1829 giving up all claims to Winnebago lands in Illinois and southern Wisconsin. It was at about this time that the Winnebago prophet White Cloud (Wabokisheik) began preaching resistance against the whites and a return to Indian ways. White Cloud would take his message and join the last attempt to stop white expansion in the Old Northwest.

Black Hawk War

In the 18th century the Sac and Fox (Mesquaki) tribes formed a confederacy. Both tribes are believed to have originally lived in what is now the southern part of Michigan. From there, they moved to the other side of Lake Michigan and settled in what is now Wisconsin and Illinois. After their confederacy defeated the

Illinois tribe in 1769, the Sac and Fox moved south, and their lands were centered along the Rock River in Illinois. In 1803, the U.S. government granted permission to Governor William Henry Harrison of Illinois to try to buy the land occupied by the Sac and Fox.

Earlier in 1803, the United States had made an agreement with the French to buy their lands west of the Mississippi River. This is known as the Louisiana Purchase. The U.S. government then decided that it would be a good idea to move the Indians of the Old Northwest to the newly acquired lands west of the Mississippi River. Harrison provided alcohol to the Sac and Fox leaders who met with him in 1804 and got them to sign a treaty in which they agreed to give up their lands in Illinois and move to the western side of the Mississippi River. The Sac and Fox leaders gave up their claim to most of what is now Wisconsin and Illinois. They received $2,000 and the promise of $1,000 in supplies each year.

Not all the Sac and Fox leaders signed or agreed with the treaty. One who disagreed was Ma-ka-tai-me-she-kia-kiak, a Sac chief who is known to history as Black Hawk. Like many other Indian leaders, Black Hawk believed, as stated in his autobiography, that the land had been a gift from the Great Spirit and could not be sold. Although Black Hawk did not agree to the 1804 treaty or other treaties that were signed after the War of 1812, he eventually moved his followers to present-day Iowa. However, he regularly returned to his village of Saukenuk (Rock Island, Illinois) on the Rock River, where the land was more fertile than in Iowa. This pattern continued for a number of years until white settlers took over Saukenuk in 1829. That year, members of Black Hawk's band lived side by side with the white squatters in their village. When Black Hawk left for the winter hunt, he told the whites he would be back in the spring.

True to his word, Black Hawk returned to Saukenuk in 1830. On June 26, 1830, a combined force of Illinois militia and federal troops marched into Saukenuk. Realizing that his force of 300 warriors could not stand against the white troops, Black Hawk led his people back across the Mississippi River. Black Hawk came back four days later under a flag of truce and signed a treaty in which he agreed to keep his followers west of the Mississippi.

Black Hawk's defiance of the white leaders in Illinois made him a popular leader among the Indians of the area. White Cloud, the Winnebago prophet, joined him with some of his

During the Black Hawk War, the Sac chief Black Hawk and his warriors fought a guerrilla-style campaign against white settlers who were moving onto lands that Black Hawk felt his people had been forced to give up. *(Library of Congress, Prints and Photographs Division [LC-USZ62-39381])*

own followers as well as warriors from the Kickapoo and the Potawatomi tribes. In spring 1832, Black Hawk and a force of 600 warriors returned to Saukenuk. A large force that included both federal troops and Illinois militia was gathered to deal with Black Hawk.

Both sides avoided a large battle for much of the spring and summer, although numerous raids against white settlers were conducted. However, on May 14, 1832, Black Hawk attempted to negotiate with the white soldiers. The warriors he sent out with a white flag of truce were fired on: Some were killed while others rushed back to warn Black Hawk. By this time all but 40 of Black Hawk's warriors had been killed or left, while there were 275 militia under the command of Major Isaiah Stillman. Despite being outnumbered by almost seven to one, Black Hawk's warriors held off Stillman's charge and then sent the remaining militia running. It is reported that they did not stop until they reached the main army camp 25 miles away. This Indian victory is known as Stillman's Run, and because of it many new recruits joined Black Hawk.

Black Hawk continually moved his force northward, and they began to suffer from exhaustion and hunger. The force that was chasing them was large, and Black Hawk's goal was to get his people back across the Mississippi, where he hoped they could find safety. On August 1, Black Hawk's people were building canoes and rafts to cross the Mississippi River near the mouth of the Bad Axe River. The steamboat *Warrior,* which had been converted into a patrol boat, came upon Black Hawk's people before they could cross the river. Black Hawk again sent out a flag of truce, which was ignored. In the ensuing battle, 23 Indians died before the *Warrior* had to head downriver to get more wood for fuel.

Black Hawk tried to convince his people that they needed to head farther north before they crossed the river. Only 50 followers left with Black Hawk. The rest stayed to finish their preparations to cross the Mississippi River. On August 3, the white troops and the refueled *Warrior* arrived just as the Indians

The Battle of Bad Axe ended the Black Hawk War of 1832. *(North Wind Picture Archives)*

were crossing the river. Caught in the middle of the river, the Indians became easy targets for the soldiers on the riverbank and on the steamboat. Approximately 300 Indians died in what is called the Battle of Bad Axe, although it was not really a battle but a slaughter.

Black Hawk evaded capture for a few more weeks, and then on August 27, he and White Cloud surrendered to federal authorities at Prairie du Chien. He was later sent to Washington, D.C., and then President Andrew Jackson sent his prisoner around to the cities in the East, where Black Hawk was displayed as a living trophy of the Indian wars. In 1833, Black Hawk dictated his autobiography. After his death in 1838, robbers dug up his grave and removed his head, which was displayed in the sideshow of a traveling carnival. The Black Hawk War marked the end of organized resistance against the government in the Old Northwest, the westernmost region of the Northeast Culture Area. Most of the Indians of the Old Northwest were forced onto a few small reservations or had to move to what was known as Indian Territory (today Oklahoma).

INDIAN LAND CESSIONS AND LIFE IN INDIAN TERRITORY

When Europeans began settling in North America, they often talked about the land as a trackless wilderness. Although much of the land was unsettled, it was all in use by the Native peoples who had long lived in North America. Every time a European built a house, cleared the land, and started a farm, it was done on land that belonged to American Indians. By the middle of the 19th century, those Indians who had survived European disease, the colonial wars, the French and Indian wars, the American Revolution, and the wars for the Old Northwest had been forced to live on a number of small reservations or had been relocated west of the Mississippi River in Indian Territory. Yet, even that arrangement was not enough for the United States as the government continued to take away Indian lands in the Northeast and the Indian Territory.

The Indian Territory was set up in 1825 on land between the Red and Missouri Rivers. The idea of moving tribes from the East to Indian Territory became official policy when the Indian Removal Act became law in 1830. By the end of the Black Hawk War, all the tribes of the Northeast were either living on small reservations or had moved to Indian Territory. (Some individual

American Indians in the United States experienced a period of tremendous transition during the 19th century as they often lost their tribal lands. Nonetheless, they did maintain some of their customs and culture. Photographed in 1890, these five Fox men are wearing traditional clothes. *(Library of Congress, Prints and Photographs Division [LC-USZ62-92960])*

LAND CESSION IN CANADA

After the French and Indian War, with the signing of the Treaty of Paris (1763), Canada became a British colony. At first the white population was still very small. Because the British needed men, and therefore the Indians in Canada, to fight against the 13 colonies to the south, the Indians were treated as allies during the American Revolution. After the Revolution, however, many Loyalists from the 13 colonies moved north, and new immigrants began to arrive from Scotland and Ireland. The pressure for Indian land caused a change in policy. In addition, many members of the Iroquois tribes that had supported the British Crown in the Revolution left New York and settled in Canada.

As Canada negotiated with what they call the First Nations for the rights to settle Indian lands, a system of reserves was set up. Tribes agreed to accept title to specific areas while retaining hunting rights to any unsettled lands in their traditional range. Throughout southern Ontario, Quebec, and the Maritime Provinces there still remain numerous Indian reserves. However, the increase in non-Indian settlement during the second half of the 19th century and early 20th century filled up much of the hunting land in these areas. The government also made an effort to impose white culture and lifestyles on its First Nations in hope of assimilating the Indian people into the general population. Today in Canada, there are many cases pending where the First Nations claim that treaties and other agreements were not upheld by the Canadian government.

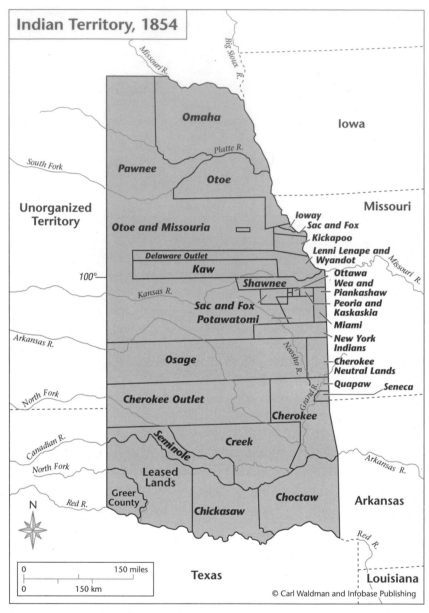

Indian Territory, 1854

Missouri R.

Big Sioux R.

Omaha

Iowa

Platte R.

South Fork

Pawnee

Otoe

Missouri

Unorganized Territory

Otoe and Missouria

Ioway
Sac and Fox
Kickapoo
Lenni Lenape and Wyandot

Missouri R.

100°

Delaware Outlet

Kaw

Ottawa
Wea and Piankashaw
Peoria and Kaskaskia

Shawnee

Kansas R.

Sac and Fox
Potawatomi

Miami

New York Indians

Arkansas R.

Osage

Neosho R.

Cherokee Neutral Lands

North Fork

Cherokee Outlet

Grand R.

Quapaw   Seneca

Cherokee

Canadian R.

Seminole

Creek

Arkansas R.

North Fork

Leased Lands

Red R.

Greer County

Chickasaw

Choctaw

Arkansas

N

Red R.

0   150 miles
0   150 km

Texas

Louisiana

© Carl Waldman and Infobase Publishing

By 1854, many tribes from the Northeast had been relocated west of the Mississippi River in what was known as Indian Territory. Over the following years, Indian Territory was greatly reduced as the government took back lands and sold or gave them to white settlers.

Indians lived off of reservations in the Northeast.) Each tribe was given a specific territory within the Indian Territory. Tribes such as the Lenni Lenape that had lived on the shores of the

Atlantic Ocean were now living in what would become Kansas and Oklahoma. Lands assigned to tribes did not always mesh well with their traditional lifestyle.

In 1824, the War Department (now called the Department of Defense) set up the Office of Indian Affairs (now called the Bureau of Indian Affairs, or BIA). This agency was transferred to the Department of the Interior in 1849. Throughout the 19th century and well into the 20th century, the mission of the Office of Indian Affairs was to supervise life on reservations and in the Indian Territory with the ultimate goal of having all Indians become a part of the mainstream white culture. This process is called assimilation. A number of strategies were used to try to achieve assimilation.

One way the Office of Indian Affairs hoped to aid in the assimilation of Native Americans was through the use of missionaries. Numerous church organizations set up missions on Indian reservations and in Indian Territory. In addition to trying

In this 1870s photograph, the chiefs from the Six Nations Reserve, located near Brantford, Ontario, and the largest reservation in Canada, study wampum belts. From left to right are Joseph Snow, Onondaga; George Henry Martin Johnson, Mohawk, father of Emily Pauline Johnson; John Buch, Onondaga; John Smoke Johnson, Mohawk, father of George Henry Martin Johnson; Isaac Hill, Onondaga; and John Senaca Johnson, Seneca. *(National Archives of Canada)*

In Indian Territory and on the reserves and reservations that remained in the Northeast, missionaries encouraged the Indians they worked with to adopt white ways and beliefs. *(National Archives, Still Picture Records [NWDNS-48-RST-5B-10])*

to convert people to Christianity, the missionaries set up schools where children learned to speak English and the ways of white culture.

As time went on, many tribes were forced to relocate again and again as the size of Indian Territory was reduced to allow more white settlement west of the Mississippi River. Some of the tribes in the Indian Territory sided with the Confederacy during the Civil War, and this was used against them to further reduce their lands. These were mainly tribes from the Southeast region of the United States, some of whom owned slaves and were more sympathetic to the Southern cause even though they had been treated terribly by whites in the Southeast. Since the overriding goal of the government was to assimilate the Indians, the

Indian agents charged with overseeing the reservations and the Indian Territory worked to help eliminate Indian culture.

For the most part, Indian policy during the 19th century was controlled by white politicians in Washington, D.C., and the various states and territories where Native Americans lived. During the presidency of Ulysses S. Grant, however, Ely S. Parker, a leader of the Seneca tribe in New York State and member of Grant's staff during the Civil War, was appointed as the first Indian commissioner of the Office of Indian Affairs. As commissioner, from 1869 to 1871, Parker helped create and then put in place President Grant's Peace Policy, as the Indian Appropriations Act of 1869 was called. Parker and the president believed that it was wrong for the United States to keep making and breaking treaties with the various tribes. Parker stated in a speech in 1869 that "great injury has been done by the government by deluding this people into the belief of their independent sovereignties, while they were at the same time dependents and wards."

The office's policy under Parker attempted to turn the jobs of Indian agents over to people selected by Protestant religious groups. The thinking was that agents selected in this manner were less likely to be corrupt and that the Indians were more likely to get what they were promised. After two years as commissioner, Parker was put on trial by Congress for alleged fraud in the operation of his job. The investigation found that he had broken rules in purchasing food for tribes in the West in an effort to keep the government's promises. He was cleared of all charges but resigned and moved to New York City with his white wife and their one daughter.

In 1887, the federal government passed the General Allotment Act, also known as the Dawes Act. This was a plan to take land ownership away from the tribes and divide it up among the individual members of the tribe. Under the Dawes Act tribal lands were surveyed and

Ely S. Parker was the first Indian to serve as commissioner of Indian affairs. He is shown here in a photograph by Mathew Brady in the 1860s. *(National Archives, Still Picture Records [NWDNS-111-B-5272])*

ELY SAMUEL PARKER
Donehogawa (1828–1895)

Before going to Washington, D.C., to work with President Ulysses S. Grant, Ely S. Parker had led a life very different from many Indians in the 19th century. He was born in 1828 on the Tonawanda Reservation near Pembroke, New York. In Seneca, he was known as Donehogawa. He attended a Baptist mission school on the reservation and later attended Yates Academy and Cayuga Academy. In the 1840s and 1850s, he was active in the fight to save tribal lands in New York. He also helped Lewis Henry Morgan with the research for his book *League of the Iroquois,* which was one of the first ethnographic studies of an Indian people. At first, Parker hoped to be a lawyer, but he was not allowed to take the bar exam because he was an Indian.

At that time, he turned his interest to engineering and went to Rensselaer Polytechnic Institute in Troy, New York. From there he took a number of engineering jobs, which included working on the Erie Canal and other major projects. As superintendent of construction of a government job in Illinois, he met and became friends with Grant. When the Civil War broke out, Parker offered to recruit a regiment of Iroquois to fight for the North. The government was not interested in arming a group of Indians and refused Parker's offer. It took his friend Grant's help for Parker to get a commission in the Army Corps of Engineers. In August 1864, Grant decided he wanted Parker on his staff and promoted him to the rank of lieutenant colonel of volunteers. As Grant's aide, Parker was given the job of writing out the terms of surrender once they were agreed upon by Grant and the commander of the Confederate troops, Robert E. Lee. Grant promoted him to brigadier general at the end of the Civil War.

Before becoming commissioner of the Office of Indian Affairs, Parker worked as a negotiator for the army in its dealing with the Sioux (Dakota, Lakota, Nakota). After resigning from his government post in 1871 and leaving Washington, he went into private business before finally taking a job with the New York City police department. When he died in 1895, he was buried near his country home in Fairfield, Connecticut. Two years later, his remains were moved to Forest Lawn Cemetery in Buffalo, New York, where he is buried near his relative Red Jacket.

indeed distributed among the members of the tribe. Once each person had received his or her allotment, according to the law, the government was free to take over any extra land. Much of the "surplus" land was sold or given to white settlers. This was a great loss to the tribes, as many acres were taken from them in this way.

Although the Dawes Act may not seem that bad in theory, in practice it was another serious blow to the American Indians. The whole idea of dividing land among the individual members of the tribe went against a basic belief of most Indians. They believed that land was not something to be owned but something that the tribe shared and took stewardship of for the good of all. In the Indian Territory and elsewhere, the land allotted to individual Indians often was the worst land available, while the best "surplus" land reverted to the government, which then turned around and sold or gave it to white settlers and land speculators. In addition, individuals were sometimes forced to take "white" names and give up tribal relations in exchange for their allotments.

A "section" of land was deemed to be 640 acres. Under the Dawes Act, Indian families received 160 acres, a quarter section. Much of the land in Indian Territory was of poor quality, and the small allotments were often not enough to support a family. The Dawes Act caused more than 90 million acres of Indian land to be lost to white settlers before it was repealed in 1934.

To further the idea of assimilation, the Carlisle Indian School was set up in 1879 in Carlisle, Pennsylvania. Indian children from reservations and the Indian Territory were sent to school there. At Carlisle, they were forced to speak only in English, dress in the style of white society, and learn skills that would help them become a part of white society. They were

Dawes Act

1887

To provide for the allotment of lands in severalty to Indians on the various reservations, and to extend the protection of the laws of the United States and the Territories over the Indians, and for other purposes.

Be it enacted . . . That in all cases where any tribe or band of Indians has been, or shall hereafter be, located upon any reservation created for their use, either by treaty stipulation or by virtue of an act of Congress or executive order setting apart the same for their use, the President of the United States be, and he hereby is, authorized, whenever in his opinion any reservation or any part thereof of such Indians is advantageous for agricultural and grazing purposes, to cause said reservation, or any part thereof, to be surveyed, or resurveyed if necessary, and to allot the lands in said reservation in severalty to any Indian located thereon in quantities as follows:

To each head of a family, one-quarter of a section;

To each single person over eighteen years of age, one-eighth of a section;

To each orphan child under eighteen years of age, one-eighth of a section; and

To each other single person under eighteen years now living, or who may be born prior to the date of the order of the President directing an allotment of the lands embraced in any reservation, one-sixteenth of a section . . .

The Carlisle Indian School operated from 1879 until 1918 in Carlisle, Pennsylvania. This photograph is of the school's 1897 graduating class. *(National Archives, Pacific Alaska Region [NRIA-WME-PHOTOS-MISC186])*

often punished for speaking their own languages and were given little contact with relatives at home. Boys were taught industrial arts and farming, while the girls were taught cooking and other domestic skills. When summer vacation time came, many students were sent to live with local families rather than being allowed to return to their Indian families. The school continued to operate until 1918. The boarding school movement was part of the government's plan to destroy Indian cultures and traditions.

As the 19th century ended, the Indians of the Northeast lived at the bottom of the social and economic structure of the country. Those who left their reservations and tried to join white society usually suffered discrimination. Those who stayed on the reservations were often forced to live on handouts from the government. As the 20th century began, it was

EMILY PAULINE JOHNSON
Tekahaionwake (1861–1913)

Emily Pauline Johnson was born on March 10, 1861, and grew up on the Six Nations Reserve near Brantford, Ontario, Canada. Her mother was English and her father, George Henry Martin Johnson, was a Mohawk chief who had been educated at English-run schools. Johnson's father was financially successful and built a large house known as "Chiefswood." During her childhood, Johnson was taught both the traditional knowledge of her Mohawk ancestors and in Indian and Canadian schools. Johnson started writing poetry as a teenager, and after her father's death in 1884, she turned to her poetry to help support herself and her mother.

A number of her poems were published in magazines and newspapers. In 1892, her career took a turn that would make her famous in Canada, the United States, and in England. At this time, she gave her first public reading of her poetry in Toronto and became an immediate success. People of the time were fascinated by the poet, who was billed as the "Mohawk Princess." Johnson would begin her readings dressed in a stylized Indian costume and then would change to an elegant evening gown at the intermission. Her poetry celebrated the beauty of Canada and spoke of the plight of American Indians.

After the Reil Rebellion of 1885, when 300 Indians fought to keep possession of their ancestral land against 8,000 Canadian soldiers, she wrote "A Cry from an Indian Wife." This poem is the lament of the wife of one of the Indian warriors who fought in the rebellion, and it was a favorite among audiences who came to her performances. Although Johnson did not take up arms to fight the injustices experienced by Indians of the time, her poetry proved the old saying that "the pen is mightier than the sword."

Many people gained a new perspective on the plight of American Indians through the poetry and performances of Emily Pauline Johnson.

A Cry from an Indian Wife

My forest brave, my Red-skin love, farewell;
We may not meet tomorrow; who can tell
What mighty ills befall our little band,
Or what you'll suffer from the white man's hand?
Here is your knife! I thought 'twas sheathed for aye.
No roaming bison calls for it today;
No hide of prairie cattle will it maim;
The plains are bare, it seeks a nobler game:
'Twill drink the life-blood of a soldier host.
Go; rise and strike, no matter what the cost.
Yet stay. Revolt not at the Union Jack,
Nor raise Thy hand against this stipling pack
Of white-faced warriors, marching West to quell
Our fallen tribe that rises to rebel.
They all are young and beautiful and good;
Curse to the war that drinks their harmless blood.
Curse to the fate that brought them from the East
To be our chiefs—to make our nation least
That breathes the air of this vast continent.
Still their new rule and council is well meant.
They but forget we Indians owned the land
From ocean unto ocean; that they stand
Upon a soil that centuries agone
Was our sole kingdom and our right alone.
They never think how they would feel today,
If some great nation came from far away,
Wresting their country from their hapless braves,
Giving what they gave us—but wars and graves.
Then go and strike for liberty and life,
And bring back honour to your Indian wife.

(continues)

(continued)

Your wife? Ah, what of that, who cares for me?
Who pities my poor love and agony?
What white-robed priest prays for your safety
here,
As prayer is said for every volunteer
That swells the ranks that Canada sends out?
Who prays for vict'ry for the Indian scout?
Who prays for our poor nation lying low?
None—therefore take your tomahawk and go.
My heart may break and burn into its core,
But I am strong to bid you go to war.
Yet stay, my heart is not the only one
That grieves the loss of husband and of son;
Think of the mothers o'er the inland seas;
Think of the pale-faced maiden on her knees;
One pleads her God to guard some sweet-
faced child
That marches on toward the North-West wild.
The other prays to shield her love from harm,

To strengthen his young, proud uplifted arm.
Ah, how her white face quivers thus to think,
Your tomahawk his life's best blood will drink.
She never thinks of my wild aching breast,
Nor prays for your dark face and eagle crest
Endangered by a thousand rifle balls,
My heart the target if my warrior falls.
O! coward self I hesitate no more;
Go forth, and win the glories of the war.
Go forth, nor bend to greed of white men's
hands,
By right, by birth we Indians own these lands,
Though starved, crushed, plundered, lies our
nation low . . .
Perhaps the white man's God has willed it so.

Source: Library and Archives of Canada Web site http://www.collectionscanada.ca/canvers-bin/entry?entry_nbr=555&l=0&page_rows=10&clctn_nbr=1.

still the goal of the government to eliminate the tribes and have the Indians disappear into mainstream white culture, as many of the different ethnic groups of immigrants already had done in the United States and Canada. The Indians themselves had no say in this plan.

8

Indians of the Northeast in the Twentieth Century

RESERVATIONS AND RESERVES

By the beginning of the 20th century, most of the Indians remaining in the Northeast lived on reservations in the United States or reserves in Canada or mixed into the general population. Numerous tribes in the Northeast no longer existed as tribal units or had been displaced to other parts of the country. Some tribes that still had members were not recognized by the government and struggled to maintain their tribal identity. In both Canada and the United States, the governments assumed a "trust relationship" with the people who lived on reserves and reservations in that the government was trusted to take care of the Indian people. This meant that the governments of the two countries acknowledged that they had a responsibility to care for the Indians within their borders. Throughout the 20th century and beyond, neither government has lived up to those responsibilities.

A reservation belongs to a tribe as a whole and has a unique legal situation. (Although within the reservation, individual Indians own their own plots.) For the most part, a reservation is not subject to the laws of the state or states in which it is located. Reservations have their own governments, laws, police, and court systems. Major crimes committed on a reservation come under the authority of the federal government. This unique situation continues on reservations today. However, the sovereignty of tribes has been a concept that has required a constant struggle. One of the most visible aspects of this struggle took place in the early 20th century between the Iroquois in Canada and the United States and the governments of the two countries.

137

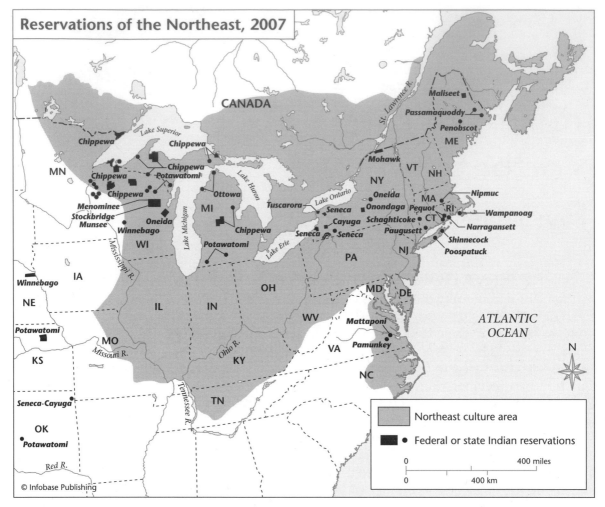

Reservations of the Northeast, 2007

CANADA

Lake Superior

Chippewa
Chippewa
MN
Chippewa
Potawatomi
Chippewa
Ottowa
Menominee
Stockbridge
Munsee
Winnebago
Oneida
WI
Potawatomi
Lake Michigan
MI
Lake Huron
Chippewa
Tuscarora
Seneca
Lake Ontario
Seneca
Seneca
Lake Erie

Maliseet
Passamaquoddy
Penobscot
ME
St. Lawrence R.
Mohawk
VT   NH
NY
Oneida
Onondaga   Pequot
Cayuga   Schaghticoke CT
Paugusett
Nipmuc
MA
RI
Wampanoag
Narragansett
Shinnecock
Poospatuck

Winnebago
IA
NE
Potawatomi
KS
MO
Missouri R.
Mississippi R.
IL   IN
OH
WV
VA
Mattaponi
Pamunkey
NJ
PA
MD   DE
KY
Ohio R.
NC
ATLANTIC
OCEAN

N

Seneca-Cayuga
OK
Potawatomi
Red R.
TN
Tennessee R.

© Infobase Publishing

Legend:

▮ Northeast culture area

▮ ● Federal or state Indian reservations

0 ———— 400 miles
0 ———— 400 km

The reservations of the Northeast represent a minuscule portion of the land that the Indians of the Northeast once controlled. Even now when tribes win land claim suits against the government, they are only rarely given back any of their land. Instead they are awarded cash settlements.

In the Jay Treaty of 1794, which was agreed to by the United States and Great Britain, the right of Indians to move freely between Canada and the United States was guaranteed. These rights were reinforced in the Treaty of Ghent, which ended the War of 1812. However, when the U.S. government passed the Indian Citizenship Act and the Immigration Act of 1924, it effectively closed the border between the United States and Canada to members of Iroquois tribes living on Canadian reserves. This act led to the creation of one of the earliest organized Indian protest movements. Chief Clinton Rickard of the Tuscarora in New York

State helped form the Indian Defense League of America (IDLA), which won reinstatement of the crossing rights in 1928. The IDLA also fought to help the Iroquois and other tribes retain their identity during the fight against termination and assimilation. The IDLA remains active in Indian issues.

In the early 20th century, the policy of assimilation continued. During these years, the U.S. federal government through the Office, and then Bureau, of Indian Affairs saw its goal

CLINTON RICKARD
(1882–1971)

Clinton Rickard was born on the Tuscarora Reservation near Niagara Falls, New York, in 1882. His father was German and left the family to join Buffalo Bill Cody's Wild West show. As a youth, Rickard lived with his Indian mother, who was aided by her family. When Rickard's father returned to the family, he was an alcoholic and abusive to his wife and children. Rickard related in his autobiography, *Fighting Tuscarora,* that he remembered having to leave the house and hide outside with his brothers as their father shot at them. Rickard pledged to himself and the Great Spirit that he would avoid alcohol and try to help people.

When he was 18, Rickard joined the army and fought in the Philippines during the Spanish-American War. After the war, he returned to the reservation and married. During this time, he worked in a quarry and farmed with his family. In the early 1920s, Rickard became the hereditary chief of the Beaver Clan and joined the Chief's Council. As a member of the council, he fought for the traditional lifestyle of the Iroquois and tried to block those who wanted change. At this time, he also became involved in the fight with the state of New York over lands that had been taken from the Iroquois.

When the U.S. government changed its immigration policy in 1924, Rickard became the leader of the movement to reinstate the right of free passage to the Iroquois on both sides of the Canadian-U.S. border. To accomplish this, in 1926, Rickard was one of the founders of what was called the Six Nations Defense League. The group soon changed its name to the Indian Defense League of America (IDLA), which is still active in Indian issues today. Rickard and the IDLA were successful in getting a bill passed in the U.S. Congress in 1928 that restored the free crossing rights of Indians. That same year, Rickard and the IDLA organized the first Border Crossing Celebration in Niagara Falls, an event that continues to this day.

The rest of his life Rickard stayed active in Indian issues, and he and the IDLA became a group that Indians throughout North America sought out for help and advice in fighting for issues that were important to them. At home, Rickard fought against the loss of Iroquois land for dams that were to be built by both the state and federal governments. Today, the IDLA continues the work begun in the 1920s by Rickard and others. His granddaughter, Jolene Rickard, carries on the family tradition as a member of the IDLA and one of the organizers of the annual crossing celebration.

Many Indians were encouraged to dress, act, and work like those who lived in the dominant white society. This group of Potawatomi men, women, and children, photographed circa 1906, wear Western clothing. *(Library of Congress, Prints and Photographs Division [LC-USZ62-132033])*

As the 20th century began, the federal government was determined to end the traditional dress and culture of all American Indians. This portrait of a Winnebago man was done circa 1904. *(Library of Congress, Prints and Photographs Division [LC-USZ62-114966])*

as eventually eliminating any and all special considerations for tribes, reservations, and the people as Indians became part of mainstream America. Many Indians resisted assimilation as they tried to maintain their traditional beliefs and Indian identities. Fortunately, in the 1930s, President Franklin D. Roosevelt promised a "New Deal" to all the people in the country suffering from the worldwide economic crisis known as the Great Depression and included the Indians living within the United States in his programs.

A NEW RESPECT FOR AMERICAN INDIANS

President Roosevelt appointed the sociologist John Collier as commissioner of Indian affairs in 1933. Collier set out to provide a New Deal for the Indians throughout the country, including those in the Northeast. The previous policy of taking away tribal land through allotments was stopped. Tribes were encouraged to write their own constitutions and form new tribal governments that could work with the Office of Indian Affairs to raise the standard of living for Indians.

Under the leadership of Collier, it looked like the office would be able to help Indians throughout the country while allowing them to maintain some of their unique cultural and ethnic identity. As optimistic as people may have been during this time, it did not last very long. Although Collier remained the head of Indian affairs until 1945, his plans and ideas were cut back as the country as a whole turned its attention to the struggle to win World War II in Europe and the Pacific. The war affected the Indians of the Northeast in a number of ways.

Many Indians joined the military. In fact, a higher percentage of Indians volunteered for military service during both World War I and II than did non-Indians. At the same time, a number of Indians left their reservations to work in industries that were making materials for the war. All these people leaving the reservations and experiencing life in the military and the industrial centers of the country created a new sense of Indian awareness.

During World War II, the visibility of American Indians was increased by their fighting gallantly in the

Under President Franklin D. Roosevelt, the government changed its policies and tried to help Indians maintain their unique cultural heritage. *(Library of Congress, Prints and Photographs Division [LC-USZ62-131953])*

LAND CLAIM VICTORIES

In 1980, the Passamaquoddy and Penobscot tribes of Maine settled a long-running dispute with the federal government. The tribes claimed that the state of Massachusetts (Maine was part of Massachusetts until 1820) had illegally taken land from the tribes in a treaty that was never ratified by the U.S. Congress. In addition, the terms of payment for the lands were never met. In the settlement that was signed by President Jimmy Carter in 1980, the tribes were granted more than $80 million. They were also allowed to buy back some of the land they had lost. The tribe invested the money in a number of businesses that benefited members of the tribe and

also created a trust fund that continues to make direct payments to members of the tribe.

Other tribes in the Northeast also filed claims against the state and federal governments. The Narragansett in Rhode Island; the Wampanoag of Martha's Vineyard, Massachusetts; the Mashantucket Pequot in Connecticut; and others were successful in receiving smaller awards from the government. Other tribes brought claims and were not successful. Overall, about 60 percent of the claims brought before the government have been settled in the Indians' favor. Some cases are still in the legal system.

THE IROQUOIS DECLARE WAR

In many ways, the unique relationship between Indian tribes and the federal government makes each tribe a sovereign nation within the boundaries of the United States. (The Iroquois even issue their own passports to members of their tribes.) Deskaheh, a Cayuga chief, went to Geneva, Switzerland, in 1922. At the time, Geneva was the home of the League of Nations (the precursor of the United Nations). Deskaheh wanted the League of Nations to recognize the sovereignty of the Iroquois. Although his appeal was denied, it brought international attention to the plight of American Indians. During both world wars, in the first half of the 20th century, the Iroquois used their sovereignty in a different manner: Each time, the Iroquois issued their own declaration of war against Germany and its allies around the world.

A high percentage of American Indians served in the U.S. military during World Wars I and II. These three female Marine Corps reservists were photographed at Camp Lejeune, North Carolina, in 1943. From left to right are Minnie Spotted Wolf, Blackfeet; Celia Mix, Potawatomi; and Violet Eastman, Chippewa. *(National Archives, Still Picture Records [208-NS-4350-2])*

war and helping with the war effort at home. After the war, there was a greater sense of what is referred to as pan-Indianism. This is a feeling that the concerns of individual Indians and tribes are part of the shared experience of all American Indians. In 1944, Native Americans from a number of different tribes, many of whom had been hired to work for the Office of Indian Affairs under Collier, joined together and formed the National Congress of American Indians.

In 1946, another change took place that would address some of the wrongs committed against the Indians of the Northeast and the rest of the country. The U.S. Congress passed a law creating an agency known as the Indian Claims Commission. The purpose of the commission, which lasted until 1978, was to process claims against the government brought by American Indians. In the 32 years it existed, the commission awarded $800 million to make up for the loss of land and other injustices committed by the government against Indians. Although the Indian Claims Commission made up for some of the previous injustices, in the 1950s, the government's policies again turned against the best interests of American Indians.

MOHAWK SKYWALKERS

In 1850, the Grand Trunk Railway built a bridge across the Saint Lawrence River and hired a number of Mohawk workers to tackle the dangerous job of erecting the bridge's iron frame. This started a long tradition of Mohawk and other Iroquois ironworkers and high steelworkers. As skywalkers, as they like to be called, the Mohawk excel. They seem fearless as they walk the narrow steel skeletons of bridges and buildings around the Northeast. Many of New York City's skyscrapers were built in part with Iroquois ironworkers and steelworkers. Many of the skywalkers moved to the city for the work. Some of those who lived in the city ended up forming a small community in Brooklyn. Others commuted to their homes on their upstate reservations on the weekends.

This type of metalwork is extremely dangerous. In 1907, 38 Mohawk workers fell 300 feet into the Saint Lawrence River when the bridge they were working on collapsed. There were only five survivors of this tragedy. Many of the Mohawk skywalkers consider their bravery walking the high steel a testament to their ancestral warrior tradition in which a man proved himself by overcoming his fears. Mohawk and other Iroquois ironworkers have worked on some of the best-known buildings in New York City, including the Empire State Building, Rockefeller Center, and the World Trade Center, which was destroyed in the terrorist attacks of September 11, 2001.

Starting in the 19th century, Mohawk and other Iroquois became ironworkers. Their ability to work high above the ground on the steel skeletons of bridges and buildings earned them the title of skywalkers. *(Library of Congress, Prints and Photographs Division [LOOK-Job 62-9888])*

TERMINATION

After World War II, the United States entered into what is called the cold war with the Soviet Union. At this time, many people in the United States became concerned that communism (a form of government in which the state controls all aspects of the life and economy of a country) would spread to the United

Ada Deer helped found the organization DRUMS in the 1960s to fight for the Menominee's tribal status. *(Bureau of Indian Affairs)*

States. Any individual or institution that seemed to suggest a communal lifestyle (as communism endorsed) was persecuted. This attitude spilled over to the reservation system and the communal lifeways of the tribes that lived on them.

In reaction to these fears, between 1954 and 1962, Congress ended the sovereign status of 61 tribes around the country. One of the largest tribes to suffer termination was the Menominee of Wisconsin. In 1961, the Menominee were forced to accept termination of their trust relationship with the federal government. The people of the tribe were told they would lose all their federal assistance if they did not agree to the change in tribal status.

Some have speculated that private companies that were interested in acquiring the rights to cut timber on the Menominee reservation worked behind the scenes in the capital for the tribe's termination. Whatever forces were involved, the Menominee set up a company to help manage the tribe's holdings and oversee the transfer of land to individual tribal members. Menominee Enterprises, Inc., soon experienced a number of problems. It took the Menominee more than 10 years and another reversal of policy in Washington before they were able to be recognized again as a tribe by the federal government. One of the reasons for the Menominee's success was the lobbying efforts of an organization known as DRUMS (Determination of Rights and Unity for Menominee Shareholders). In the early 1970s, a number of other Northeast tribes were able to reverse their termination. This included the Modoc, Peoria, Ottawa, and Wyandot (Huron).

INDIAN ACTIVISM

The 1960s was a time of turmoil in the United States. Protesters took to the streets to demonstrate against the country's involvement in the war in Vietnam. At about the same time, African Americans were marching and demonstrating in order to receive the equal treatment under the law that they deserved. Although they were a much smaller group, American Indians also became more active in making the public aware of many of

ADA DEER AND DRUMS

One of the founders of DRUMS was Ada Deer. Deer was born in 1935 on the Menominee Reservation in Wisconsin. She grew up in a one-room log cabin on the reservation that did not have central heat or running water. Deer's father was a Menominee who worked at the tribe's sawmill and who had been sent off the reservation to a boarding school when he was a child. Her mother, Constance Wood Deer, was from a wealthy white family in Philadelphia. Constance had become a nurse and gone to work for the Office of Indian Affairs, which sent her to Wisconsin to help provide medical services to the Menominee.

Ada Deer was a talented and serious student who won a college scholarship. The scholarship was sponsored by the University of Wisconsin at Madison and by the Menominee tribe. It allowed Deer the opportunity to attend the university, where in 1957 she received her bachelor's degree. She then went on to Columbia University, where she earned a master's degree in social work. As a social worker, she returned to the upper Midwest and worked for a time in Minneapolis, which had a large, poor Indian population.

In 1964, Deer went to work for the Bureau of Indian Affairs (BIA) in Minneapolis but found working for the government bureaucracy extremely difficult. (The Office of Indian Affairs had been renamed after World War II.) After she left the BIA, she worked for a number of different organizations. She then returned to what had been the Menominee Reservation to help found DRUMS (Determination of Rights and Unity for Menominee Shareholders), which would lead the fight for the restoration of the Menominee's tribal status, terminated in 1961. When the tribe was restored in 1973, Deer served as the tribe's chairperson. During her time as chairperson, she oversaw the writing of the tribe's new constitution.

(continues)

Like many Indians of his generation, the father of future Menominee activist Ada Deer was sent off the reservation to a boarding school where he was taught that Indian ways were wrong. *(Library of Congress, Prints and Photographs Division [LC-USZ62-72450 and LC-USZ62-47082])*

(continued)

In 1977, Deer went to work at the University of Wisconsin–Madison as a lecturer. Over the next two decades, she remained active in state and national politics. She twice ran unsuccessfully for the office of secretary of state for Wisconsin. In 1992, she tried to unseat an incumbent Republican member of the House of Representatives. Although she did not win, she did gain the attention of Bill Clinton who at the time was running for his first term as president of the United States.

In 1993, President Clinton asked Deer to serve as the assistant secretary of the interior for Indian affairs. This put her in charge of the bureaucracy she had been unable to deal with earlier in her life. As the head of the BIA, Deer worked tirelessly to help Indian people around the country. During the four years she headed the BIA, 180 tribes were able to expand their self-governance, and 145 agreements between states and tribes allowing gaming on tribal lands were approved. In addition, many tribes were able to gain control of the education systems on their reservations.

Deer left her position at the BIA at the end of President Clinton's first term and returned to the University of Wisconsin–Madison, where she is the director of the American Indian studies program.

---

the injustices they had suffered since the first Europeans arrived in North America and pushing for change in the way they were being treated.

By this point, the vast majority of American Indians lived west of the Mississippi River, although the Northeast saw more than its proportional share of Indian activism during this time. In 1961, the American Indian Chicago Conference was held, and 67 tribes sent approximately 500 delegates to discuss how Indians could work together on common issues. The conference issued a Declaration of Indian Purpose. One of the major points of the declaration was that Indians needed to have a greater say in the governmental policies that affected them. Some of the more radical younger members of the conference went on to form groups that led a number of protests.

In 1968, the best-known group of the time was founded in Minneapolis, Minnesota, by five members of the Northeast Anishinabe tribe (Chippewa/Ojibway), Dennis Banks, George Mitchell, Clyde Bellecourt, Eddie Benton-Banai, and Mary Jane Wilson. The group was called the American Indian Movement (AIM). It initially began to combat police brutality against Indians but went on to advocate on larger issues. AIM became the most militant of the Indian groups.

Since the 1960s AIM and other Indian groups have participated in numerous protests around the country. AIM's best-known protest action was the takeover of Alcatraz Island in San Francisco Bay in 1969. In the past, Alcatraz had been used as a federal prison. To gain attention for the mistreatment of all Indians, members of AIM occupied it for 19 months before they were removed by federal marshals. In the Northeast, there were numerous protests as well.

Following the example of the "capture" of Alcatraz, in 1970, Indians in the Northeast took over the *Mayflower II* (the replica of the ship in which the Pilgrims arrived at Plymouth) at its berth in Plymouth, Massachusetts. There was also an attempt to occupy Ellis Island in New York harbor. One successful occupation took place in the Adirondack Mountains of New York. In 1974, 200 members of the Akwesasne Mohawk moved onto a piece of land at Eagle Bay on Moss Lake. They claimed this was part of their original territory, and they wanted it back from the state. The Mohawk referred to the 612-acre area as Ganienkeh. As a result of their occupation of Ganienkeh, the Mohawk were able to negotiate for reservation lands at Altona and Schuyler Lakes in Clinton County, New York, in 1977.

The protest movement happened on both sides of the border with Canada. In 1988, the Mohawk on the Kahnawake Reserve blocked roads and a bridge on the reserve that were used by many non-Indians as a route to Montreal. The reason for this protest was the arrest of some tribal members for bringing in cigarettes from the United States without paying Canadian

URBAN INDIANS

The founders of the American Indian Movement (AIM) lived in the city of Minneapolis and in many ways spoke for the plight of all urban Indians. After World War II, rural people from all over the United States of all ethnicities began leaving their hometowns. They headed for the urban centers of the country in hopes of making a better life for themselves and their families. Prior to World War II, less than 10 percent of American Indians lived in cities. The censuses since 1940 have shown an ever-increasing percentage of Indians living in cities. As of the 2000 census, more than 63 percent of American Indians lived in urban areas. In the Northeast region, Chicago, Buffalo, New York City; Boston; and Washington, D.C., are some of the cities with substantial Indian populations, and more Indians live in New York City than in any other U.S. city. Urban Indians, like those Indians who live on reservations and reserves, often live in poverty and experience numerous problems because of it.

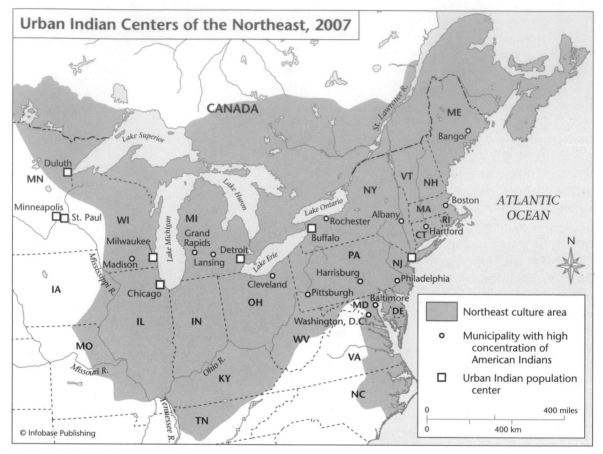

Urban Indian Centers of the Northeast, 2007

CANADA

ME
Bangor

Lake Superior

Duluth
MN

VT
NH

NY

Boston
ATLANTIC
OCEAN

Minneapolis
St. Paul

Lake Ontario
Albany
MA
RI

WI
Rochester
CT
Hartford

MI
Buffalo

Milwaukee
Grand
Rapids
Detroit
PA

Madison
Lansing
Harrisburg
NJ
Philadelphia

IA
Chicago
Cleveland
Pittsburgh
Baltimore

OH
MD
DE

IL
IN
Washington, D.C.

MO
WV

VA

Ohio R.
KY

NC

TN

© Infobase Publishing

Legend:
- Northeast culture area
- ○ Municipality with high concentration of American Indians
- ☐ Urban Indian population center

0   400 miles
0   400 km

More than half of all American Indians now live in urban areas. New York City has the largest Indian population of any urban area. The other urban areas in the Northeast with significant Indian populations are shown here.

import taxes. The Mohawk claimed that their treaty allowed them to cross the international boundary freely. Two years later, Mohawk from the same reserve ended up in a standoff with Quebec police when they protested the building of a golf course on land that had been a tribal burial ground. There was shooting from both sides, and one police officer was killed.

In a similar incident in 1995 between the Chippewa and the Ontario police, one protester, Dudley George, was killed and a 13-year-old boy was wounded. Both George and the boy were unarmed. In this instance, a number of protesters were jailed. The police officer, who was in charge and ultimately responsible for the shooting of the two protesters, was only sentenced to perform community service.

Despite the fact that the colonial and the U.S. governments systematically took almost all of the Indians' land in the Northeast, the government continues to take additional Indian land when it needs more. Twice in the 20th century, the Seneca have lost land to the government. In the late 1950s a dam was proposed across the Allegheny River that would flood thousands of acres of Seneca land. The Seneca organized numerous protests, but the Army Corps of Engineers nonetheless started building the dam (Kinzua Dam) in 1964. When the dam was completed in 1965, 10,500 acres of the Seneca Reservation disappeared under water. This included land given to Chief Cornplanter by George Washington. Then, in 1985, the Seneca tried to prevent the expansion of an expressway through their Allegany Reservation. The leaders of the Seneca claimed that the land had been sold illegally to the state in 1976.

Although numerous protests have taken place since the 1960s and gains have been made by the Indians of the Northeast, as a group they continue to be at the bottom of the economic ladder in the United States and Canada. As the 20th century came to a close, many tribes hoped that they could improve life and provide jobs for their people by allowing gambling on their reservations.

INDIAN CASINOS

Due to the unique nature of reservations, many tribes have been able to open all sorts of gaming enterprises on their land. Everything from high-stakes bingo to the largest casino in the world can be found on Indian lands in the Northeast. There are a total of 47 gaming establishments operated by tribes in the Northeast. Six of them are in New York, 17 in Michigan, 21 in Wisconsin, two in Connecticut, and one in Maine. Foxwoods Resort and Casino in Connecticut, which is operated by the Mashantucket Pequot tribe is the largest and offers a full line of games. Some of the smallest places offer only high-stakes bingo.

The experience with gaming has been mixed for the tribes that have turned to it as a source of revenue. Some tribes, such as the Mashantucket Pequot and the Oneida, the latter of which operate both the Turning Stone Resort and Casino and the Oneida Nation Bingo, have been able to locate their gaming establishments where they are easily accessible to large numbers of people. These enterprises have been very successful.

In fact, the Oneida have done so well that they no longer accept federal assistance for the tribe and were able to donate

$10 million to the new National Museum of the American Indian in Washington, D.C. On other reservations, the gaming industry has done little to help the tribes. Poor locations in rural areas have been unable to attract the number of customers that were originally expected. Casinos have also been controversial among members of various tribes.

Many Indians who want to preserve traditional tribal values believe that casinos and bingo parlors have a negative influence on the tribe. The conflict among the members of the Saint Regis Mohawk tribe over the opening of the Akwesasne Mohawk Casino in Hogansburg, New York, which is located in the northern part of the state along the Saint Lawrence River, ended in the death of two tribal members in May 1990. Some of the members of the traditionalist faction were so upset by the casino that in 1993 they bought land along the Mohawk River and established a new Mohawk community. They call their community Kanatsiohareke and try to live in a traditional manner as much as possible.

Operated by the Mashantucket Pequot tribe, Foxwoods Resort and Casino in Connecticut is the largest of its kind. *(AP Images/Carla M. Cataldi)*

CULTURAL RENEWAL

At the end of the 20th century, the Mohawk at Kanatsiohareke were not the only Indians who took a renewed interest in their own culture and tradition. Many other Indians as well are working to keep their native languages alive. There has also been a revival in Indian arts and crafts that has found a ready market among the non-Indian population that has come to appreciate the beauty and value of Indian ways. The creation of the National Museum of the American Indian in 1989 and the completion of its new facility in Washington, D.C., in 2004 showcases the culture of North America's first inhabitants. As the 21st century unfolds, the future for the Indians of the Northeast is more positive than it was at the beginning of the last century. However, American Indians throughout the United States and Canada still face numerous challenges.

9

Northeast Indians Today

♛ CASINOS AND OTHER ENTERPRISES

The success of the casinos and bingo halls during the 1990s created a rush of tribes and states looking to Indian gaming enterprises as a way to solve tribal, state, and local financial problems. Casinos such as Turning Stone in New York and Mohegan Sun and Foxwoods in Connecticut have collectively generated billions of dollars in revenue. The Connecticut casinos have also provided much needed revenue for the state of Connecticut through an agreement that gives the state a percentage of the profits. They are also some of the largest employers in the state.

In Connecticut, Maine, New Jersey, and New York, additional Indian casinos have been proposed by tribes, but in at least two cases, local non-Indian communities went looking for tribes that would bring a casino to their towns. Wildwood, New Jersey, is a beach community along the Jersey shore that has suffered economically as gambling in nearby Atlantic City has drawn off most of its tourist business. New Jersey limits gambling to Atlantic City, and the town leaders in Wildwood came up with a unique plan to get around the New Jersey law: They decided to look for an Indian tribe to partner with the town.

They ran into a problem because there are no federally recognized tribes in New Jersey. The last of the Lenni Lenape had been forced off their land by the state in the 1830s, and most joined other members of the tribe to the west. The town of Wildwood sought to reverse that trend and offered to give the Lenni Lenape of Anadarko, Oklahoma, two acres in the center of town. Any land that a tribe owns can become part of its reservation and then is no longer subject to state law. But in this instance, Wildwood got more than it bargained for.

The Lenni Lenape saw the offer from Wildwood as an opening to press a claim for lands that were taken from them illegally in the 1830s and before. In addition, the Lenni Lenape have turned their attention to Pennsylvania, where they were also forced to leave during the colonial and the early years of the United States. Pennsylvania is a densely populated state without any casino gambling. The Lenni Lenape have filed suit over a 315-acre parcel that they claim was illegally taken from them. As the suit goes forward, the Lenni Lenape are using it as leverage to try to pressure the state to grant them the right to purchase land and open casinos near Philadelphia, Pittsburgh, and some other locations around the state.

New York State, which missed out on getting any income from Turning Stone, is now working with tribes to build more casinos. The Seneca are building a casino near Buffalo and have already opened one in Niagara Falls. The Cayuga are now working on a deal to build a casino in the Catskills Mountains, where a once-flourishing tourist industry has fallen on economic hard times. This is the other instance where a community went looking for a tribe. A number of these new casino efforts are backed by large development companies that partner with the tribes and often spend millions of dollars to lobby federal, state, and local governments to help arrange agreements to build casinos. These companies then provide the capital to build and operate the new casinos as they become partners with the tribes involved.

In Maine, a special referendum that would have allowed for an Indian-operated casino in the tourist-rich southern part of the state was recently defeated. Other tribes in Connecticut and Massachusetts are also considering additional

Chief Wildred "Eagle Heart" Greene of the Seaconke Wampanoag tribe first filed a lawsuit in early 2003 claiming 34 square miles of land in northeastern Rhode Island based on a 1661 deed. Although the claim has been dismissed, the tribe continues to appeal the decision. Greene holds the paperwork in this March 2003 photograph. *(AP Images/Stew Milne)*

casinos. The profits from casinos as well as land claim settlements have led to two parallel activities: a renewed effort by many unrecognized tribes in the Northeast to gain federal tribal status and a search for investment opportunities by tribes with profits from casinos or land claims.

The Passamaquoddy of Maine, which shared in an $80 million land claim settlement with the Penobscot, have brought a number of businesses to their reservation located in the far southeastern corner of the state. Some of the casino profits from the Oneida and Forest County Potawatomi of Wisconsin and two California tribes have been invested in a new hotel in Washington, D.C.: The 13-story Residence Inn by Marriot has 223 suites and is only three blocks from the new National Museum of the American Indian, which opened in September 2004. The museum is expected to attract 6 million visitors a year. Meanwhile, the high stakes involved in land claims and casinos have brought new urgency to a number of Northeast tribes that are still seeking recognition from the federal government.

TRIBAL RECOGNITION

Without federal recognition, a tribe cannot benefit from the sovereign status that recognized tribes have. Tribes from Vermont to Virginia are working to gain or regain federal status. The federal government has a long and involved process for recognizing tribes, and not all the tribes that apply make it to approval. One tribe that recently failed in its attempt for recognition was the Golden Hill Paugussett near Bridgeport, Connecticut. The Bureau of Indian Affairs (BIA), successor to the Office of Indian Affairs, stated that the tribe failed to prove that it was directly descended from the original tribe at Golden Hill. The tribe was planning to build a casino in Bridgeport and had received millions of dollars from developers to help in their attempt to gain recognition.

In another case along the border of Connecticut and Massachusetts, two separate bands that were historically related ended up with differing results. The Hassanamisco Band of the Nipmuc and the Chaubunagungamaug Band of Nipmuck began their attempts at recognition in 1980, long before anyone had opened an Indian casino. Finally, in 2001, the government handed down a decision. The Nipmuc were granted federal status. The Nipmuck were denied, although they have appealed the decision. The government claimed that the Nipmuck did not show that it had continuously been a separate

Although recognized as a tribe by the state of Connecticut, the Golden Hill Paugussett have to date failed in their attempts to be recognized by the U.S. government. In this 2004 photograph, Shoran Piper sits on the steps of a building on the Golden Hill Paugussett Reservation in Trumbull, Connecticut. (*AP Images/Douglas Healey*)

tribe throughout history. The Nipmuc are now attempting to open Massachusetts's first casino. But even without the casino, recognition brings many benefits with it. Recognized tribes have special status and receive many legal and financial benefits.

The remnants of the 32 bands that made up the Powhatan Confederacy in Virginia have lived an almost invisible existence in southern Virginia for centuries. After the Indians surrendered to British colonial officials, they and their descendants lived quietly without any formal acknowledgment from the state or federal government. Based on the Racial Integrity Act of 1924, Virginia even refused to recognize them as Indians on their birth certificates until 1967, marking them as either white or "negro." Now, the 16,000 Indians in Virginia are seeking federal status.

In Vermont, history textbooks approved by the state went so far as to assert that no Indians had ever lived there. However, the Western Abenaki still live in their traditional homesite of Swanton, Vermont. Under the leadership of their controversial leader Homer St. Francis, they have confronted the state and are working toward recognition.

FACING THE FUTURE

Those tribes that have invested land claims money wisely or have income from successful gaming establishments have done much to improve social and economic conditions for the people living on their reservations. Investments in schools, medical facilities, cultural centers, and other services have improved conditions for people. Tribes such as the Pequot have made sure that their tribal members have jobs at Foxwoods or in other tribal enterprises.

However, for the majority of American Indians in the Northeast region, especially those who live in the cities or on reservations without profitable casinos or who belong to unrecognized tribes, the historic economic and health-related problems still continue. The 2000 U.S. Census counted 281,412,906 people in the United States, and only 1.5 percent, or 4,119,301 people, reported that they were all or part American Indian or Alaska Native. More than half that group, 2,475,956 people, stated that they were all American Indian. In the Northeast region, the census reported 884,029 American Indians.

Almost every category measured by the 2000 census shows that American Indians are less well off than the population as a whole. For instance, in New York State, the median value of owner-owned houses is $148,700. Among the Iroquois in New York, the median value of houses is $73,200. The census area that includes New York City, Long Island, northern New Jersey, and part of Connecticut reported in 2000 a median income for all males holding full-time jobs of $45,115, while the

Indian Population in the Northeast, 2000 Census

States	Indian Population
Connecticut	24,488
Delaware	6,069
District of Columbia	4,775
Illinois	73,161
Indiana	39,263
Kentucky	24,552
Maine	13,156
Maryland	39,437
Massachusetts	38,050
Michigan	124,412
New Hampshire	7,885
New Jersey	49,104
New York	171,581
Ohio	76,075
Pennsylvania	52,650
Rhode Island	10,725
Vermont	6,396
Virginia	52,864
Wisconsin	69,386

Fewer than 1 million Indians live in the Northeast today. New York and Michigan are the states in the region with the largest Indian populations.

male American Indians and Alaska Natives holding full-time jobs living in the same area had a median income of $30,943.

When looking further into the earnings of American Indians in the Northeast, the recently recognized Nipmuc tribe is one of the poorest, with a median income of $18,500 for adult males who held full-time, year-round jobs; members of the same group among the Tonawanda Band of Seneca earn even less, $12,063 per year. The only tribe exceeding the area's overall median income is the casino-rich Mashantucket Pequot, whose 63 male members who reported they held full-time, year-round employment had a median income of more than $100,000.

Nationally, 12.4 percent of the U.S. population lives below the poverty level. Among the entire American Indian population, 25.8 percent—more than double the national percentage—live in poverty. The Iroquois as a whole are doing better than most Indians but still have 19 percent living in poverty. Some Iroquois groups, such as the Cayuga Nation, are doing worse, however, with 29.6 percent below the poverty level. For households where the head is an Indian woman with children, the percentage living below the poverty level jumps up to 45.9 percent.

The Ramapough Mountain Band of Lenni Lenape in northern New Jersey have not been successful in attempts to pursue federal recognition. This photograph shows Ramapough Mountain Indians protesting outside the Interior Department in Washington, D.C., on November 13, 1995. *(AP Images/Charles Tasnadi)*

Similar differences exist in education as well. In the U.S. Census Bureau's Northeast region, 81.6 percent of the population as a whole over age 25 have at least graduated from high school. Among American Indians and Alaska Natives in the same region, only 69.3 percent have graduated from high school. For some groups, such as the unrecognized Ramapough Mountain Band of the Lenni Lenape who live in northern New Jersey, only 55.2 percent reported completing high school. Among the Iroquois in the region, where the tribes with casino income have put resources into improving education for their people, 77 percent of the population over 25 has completed high school.

American Indians also face a number of health-related problems. Some of these problems are related to the relative poverty of American Indians, while others, such as alcoholism and diabetes, have a genetic component as well. The rate of alcoholism among Indians is higher than for any other ethnic group and is a major problem on many reservations. Diabetes is a growing problem among Indians. Approximately one in eight adult Indians has diabetes. Among whites, the rate is about half that.

A BETTER TOMORROW

Despite the challenges facing tribes and individual Indians, it appears that Indians in the Northeast are in many cases finding a way to improve their living conditions while retaining their unique cultural differences. There are projects such as the Faithkeepers School started in 1998 by Lehman and Sandy Dowdy of the Seneca tribe where traditional beliefs and the Seneca language are being taught to its students. Nationally, it has been recognized that among young American Indians, an interest in and understanding of their cultural heritage is helping youth avoid drug and alcohol abuse or maintain their recovery from it.

The Red Lake Band of Chippewa in Minnesota started a program in the 1980s where learning to respect cultural traditions and participation in group activities has served to give young people on the reservation a feeling of belonging. Through such programs as their summer cultural immersion camp, many young Chippewa have come to learn the Ojibwa language. Similar programs exist among many other tribes and are helping young American Indians have a greater respect for themselves and their heritage.

LOUISE ERDRICH
(1954–)

One reason that many non-Indians are more aware today of the plight of American Indians is because of a growing group of publicly recognized Indian writers and artists. Through art and literature, they tell the story of American Indians from their own unique perspectives. One influential person in this group is the best-selling author Louise Erdrich. Many of her numerous books tell the fictionalized story of life on and around the Turtle Mountain Reservation of the Chippewa in Minnesota.

Louise Erdrich was born in 1954 in Little Falls, Minnesota, and was the eldest of seven children. Her father is of German-American descent, and her mother is part French and part Chippewa of the Turtle Mountain Band. Erdrich's father and mother both worked at the Bureau of Indian Affairs school in Wahpeton, North Dakota. Erdrich's grandfather on his mother's side was tribal chairman on the Turtle Mountain Reservation, and Erdrich spent a lot of time with relatives on the reservation when she was growing up.

Erdrich was encouraged from an early age to pursue her interest in writing. Her father would give her five cents for each story. Her mother helped her by making construction paper covers for her writings. Erdrich has said that one of the reasons she feels compelled to tell stories about the experiences of the Chippewa and the other characters in her books is because her Indian relatives were all great storytellers. She claims that most conversations with her relatives would end up with one of them telling her a story. Many of these stories were about the history and culture of her Chippewa ancestors.

Although a naturally good writer, Erdrich improved her skills as one of the women in the first coeducational class of Dartmouth College in 1972. After Dartmouth, she earned a master's degree in writing from John Hopkins University. Despite the fact that Erdrich won a number of awards for her writing while still a student, it was not until 1984 that her first novel, *Love Medicine,* and her first book of poetry, *Jacklight,* were published.

In 1981, Erdrich married Michael Dorris, who had been one of her professors at Dartmouth in the 1970s. Dorris was part Modoc (a tribe from northern California and southern Oregon) and brought three adopted Indian children to the marriage. All of Dorris's adopted children were born with fetal alcohol syndrome, caused by the mother consuming large amounts of alcohol during pregnancy. In addition, the couple had three daughters during their marriage, which began to break up in 1996 and ended on April 15, 1997, when Dorris committed suicide. Erdrich credits Dorris with contributing greatly to her success, as he collaborated with her on much of her work and acted as her agent. Erdrich is still writing and owns a bookstore in Minneapolis, which she runs with the help of her three daughters.

PUBLISHED WORKS OF LOUISE ERDRICH:

Poetry
Baptism of Desire, 1989
Jacklight, 1984
Original Fire, 2003

Novels
The Antelope Wife, 1998
The Beet Queen, 1986

(continues)

(continued)

The Blue Jay's Dance, 1995

The Crown of Columbus, with Michael Dorris, 1991

Four Souls, 2004

Last Report on the Miracles at Little No Horse, 2003

Love Medicine, 1984; expanded edition, 1993

Master Butchers Singing Club, 2003

Tracks, 1988

Short Stories

The Bingo Palace, 1994

Tales of Burning Love, 1996

Books for Young Readers

Birchbark House, 1999

Game of Silence, 2005

Grandmother's Pigeon, 1996

Range Eternal, 2002

In Boston, Massachusetts, another type of victory was won by American Indians in 2005. Since 1996, the Muhheconnew National Confederacy, which represents a group of Northeastern tribes, had been advocating for the repeal of a law passed in Boston in 1675. The law, which prohibits Indians from being in Boston, was enacted in hopes of preventing attacks during King Philip's War. Although the law had been overruled by the state constitution passed in 1790, it was still on the books. When Unity, a group that represents minority member journalists including American Indians, said it would not consider Boston for its 9,000-member convention in 2008 because of this law, it was finally, successfully repealed.

One of the most promising events for American Indians in recent years was the opening of the Smithsonian Institution's National Museum of the American Indian in September 2004 on the Mall in Washington, D.C. This museum displays the art and history of American Indians from their own perspective. The exhibits in the museum were created with input from American Indian curators and representatives from tribes from the Arctic to the southern tip of Chile. The museum provides non-Indian visitors to the museum the opportunity to come to a better understanding of exactly who American Indians are and what has happened to them over the more than 500 years since Europeans began to arrive in their territory. The museum will add to everyone's growing appreciation of what has been done to the first Americans and celebrate all they have accomplished.

Red Chief Stronghorse of the New Jersey Cherokee Nation walks in the dedication ceremony for the National Museum of the American Indian in Washington, D.C., on September 21, 2004. *(AP Images/Pablo Martinez Monsivais)*

The opening of the museum included a six-day First Americans Festival with 300 participants from more than 50 tribes. One of the highlights of the opening ceremonies was the Native Nations Procession, where 25,000 people representing more than 500 tribes walked from the main Smithsonian museum building (the Castle) to the U.S. Capitol. Many of the people in the procession wore traditional clothing in the styles of tribes from all corners of the Americas. The museum will continue to make more people aware of the American Indians, their history, their culture, their present, and their future.

As the Indians of the Northeast go forward, the expansion of casino gambling and other types of economic development for tribes in the region will continue to provide money to relieve some of the economic problems. Recognition of additional tribes will also help provide needed services to Indians. American Indians were here thousands of years before the coming of Europeans. Despite efforts over a long period of time to eliminate them, the Indians of the Northeast have survived. They still have problems to solve, but solutions exist, and there will be Indians in the Northeast for many generations to come.

⚔ Time Line ⚔

12,000 B.C.
Paleo-Indians' range expands into the Northeast.

10,500–6000
The first evidence of Clovis points is found in the Northeast.

6000–3000
The Archaic tradition emerges in the Northeast with the use of pottery.

3000–300
With the development of agriculture, late Archaic tradition develops in the Northeast.

300 B.C.–A.D. 1600
Woodland culture is present throughout the Northeast.

A.D. 1000
Vikings live in the Canadian Maritimes on the Atlantic coast.

1497
John Cabot explores the Northeast coast.

1524
Giovanni da Verrazano sails along the Northeast coast.

1534–1541
Jacques Cartier makes three trips to North America.

1585
English colonists at Roanoke (in present-day North Carolina) disappear. Some believe survivors joined Indians in Virginia.

1607

Jamestown is founded, and Powhatan helps the settlers by trading and giving them food.

1616–1619

Disease epidemics sweep through the Northeast, killing thousands of Indians.

1620

Plymouth colony is established. Wampanoag leader Massasoit provides food and other help.

1637

The Pequot War is fought in New England.

1640

The Pig War, Kieft's War, is fought in New Netherland.

1675–1676

King Philip's War is waged in New England.

1689–1697

King William's War takes place between the English and French.

1702–1713

Queen Anne's War is fought between the English and French.

1711–1713

The Tuscarora War takes place in North Carolina between the Tuscarora and European settlers.

1744–1748

King George's War is fought between the English and French.

1755–1762

The French and Indian War starts in North America and later spreads to Europe. The French lose and give up Canada to the English.

1790

Little Turtle's War is waged in the Ohio River valley.

1811

The Shawnee leader Tecumseh is defeated at the Battle of Tippecanoe.

1813

Tecumseh is killed during the Battle of the Thames in Ontario.

1824

The Office of Indian Affairs is established.

1825

A separate Indian Territory is established west of the Mississippi River.

1827

The Winnebago leader Red Bird and his followers are defeated by Illinois and federal troops.

1830

The Indian Removal Act is passed in Congress.

1832

The Black Hawk War is fought in Illinois and Wisconsin.

1879

The Carlisle Indian School in Carlisle, Pennsylvania, is founded.

1887

The General Allotment Act, known as the Dawes Act, establishing many new Indian reservations, is signed into law.

1922

Deskaheh, a Cayuga chief, asks the League of Nations in Geneva, Switzerland, to recognize the sovereignty of the Iroquois.

1946

The Indian Claims Commission is established.

1947

The Office of Indian Affairs is officially renamed the Bureau of Indian Affairs (BIA).

1961

The Menominee of Wisconsin lose their tribal status.

1970

American Indian Movement (AIM) members take over the *Mayflower II* in Plymouth, Massachusetts.

1972
The Menominee Restoration Act is passed, reestablishing the Menominee as a federally recognized tribe.

1974
The Akwesasne Mohawk take over Eagle Bay at Moss Lake in the Adirondack region of New York.

1980
The Passamaquoddy and Penobscot of Maine receive $80 million to settle their land claims.

1988
The Kahnawake Mohawk block roads and a bridge in a dispute over the Mohawk right to move freely between the United States and Canada.

1990
A disagreement over casinos between groups of Mohawk results in two deaths and later in the establishment of a new community of Mohawk.

1995
Ramapough Mountain Indians seek federal recognition.

1998
Faithkeeper's School started by Seneca to teach language and traditional beliefs.

2001
Nipmuc are granted federal status as a recognized Indian tribe.

2004
The National Museum of the American Indian opens in Washington, D.C.

2005
Boston repeals 1685 law prohibiting Indians from entering the city.

2007
In June, members of the Mohawk and five other tribes meet in New Hampshire to protest climate change and global warming.

Historical Sites and Museums

UNITED STATES
Connecticut

MASHANTUCKET

Mashantucket Pequot Museum and Research Center The tribally owned Mashantucket Pequot Museum opened in 1998 with 85,000 square feet of exhibit space.

> *Address:* 110 Pequot Trail, P.O. Box 3180, Mashantucket, CT 06338
> *Phone:* 800-411-9671
> *Web Site:* http://www.pequotmuseum.org

Indiana

BATTLE GROUND

Museum at Prophetstown The Prophetstown Living History Village includes a council house and wigwams.

> *Address:* 3549 Prophetstown Trail, P.O. Box 331, Battle Ground, IN 47920
> *Phone:* 765-567-4700
> *Web Site:* http://www.prophetstown.org/nativeamerican.html

INDIANAPOLIS

Eiteljorg Museum of American Indian and Western Art The Eiteljorg Museum is dedicated to the art of the American Indian and of the West.

> *Address:* 500 West Washington Street, Indianapolis, IN 46204
> *Phone:* 317-636-9378
> *Web Site:* http://www.eiteljorg.org

Maine

BAR HARBOR

Abbe Museum The collections of the Abbe Museum include 50,000 Indian artifacts from the past 10,000 years.

> *Address:* P.O. Box 286, Bar Harbor, ME 04609
> *Phone:* 207-288-3519
> *Web Site:* http://www.abbemuseum.org

INDIAN ISLAND

Penobscot Nation Museum The Penobscot Nation Museum houses both traditional and modern Penobscot and Abenaki materials and art.

> *Address:* 5 Downstreet Street, Indian Island, ME 04468
> *Phone:* 207-827-4153
> *Web Site:* http://www.penobscotnation.org/museum/index.htm

PERRY

Waponahki Museum The Waponahki Museum houses displays of American Indian artifacts.

> *Address:* Pleasant Point, Perry, ME 04667
> *Phone:* 207-853-4001
> *Web Site:* http://www.mainemuseums.org/htm/museumdetail.
>   php3?orgID=1607

Maryland

SUITLAND

National Museum of the American Indian Cultural Resources Center For the most part the American Indian materials collected by George Gustav Heye and formerly held at the Heye Museum in New York City have been moved to the Suitland Cultural Resources Center. Tours are available.

> *Address*: 4220 Silver Hill Road, Suitland, MD 20746
> *Phone:* 301-238-1435
> *Web Site:* http://www.nmai.si.edu

Massachusetts

CAMBRIDGE

Peabody Museum of Archaeology and Ethnology The Peabody Museum, founded in 1866, houses a large collection of American Indian artifacts.

> *Address:* 11 Divinity Avenue, Cambridge, MA 02138
> *Phone:* 617-496-1027
> *Web Site:* http://www.peabody.harvard.edu

PLYMOUTH

Hobbamock's Homesite Hobbamock's Homesite at Plimoth Plantation shows how a Wampanoag family would have lived in the early 17th century.

> *Address:* Plimoth Plantation, 137 Warren Avenue, Plymouth, MA 02360
> *Phone:* 508-746-1622
> *Web Site:* http://www.plimoth.org/visit/what/hobbamock.asp

New Hampshire

WARNER

Mount Kearsarge Indian Museum The Mount Kearsarge Indian Museum Education and Cultural Center houses exhibits and hosts programs designed to increase awareness of American Indian history and culture.

> *Address:* Kearsarge Mountain Road, P.O. Box 142, Warner, NH 03278
> *Phone:* 603-456-3244
> *Web Site:* http://www.indianmuseum.org

New York

HOWES CAVE

Iroquois Indian Museum The Iroquois Indian Museum offers exhibits of Iroquois culture and art.

> *Address:* 324 Caverns Road, P.O. Box 7, Howes Cave, NY 12092
> *Phone:* 518-296-8949
> *Web Site:* http://www.iroquoismuseum.org

NEW YORK CITY

National Museum of the American Indian George Gustav Heye Center The George Gustav Heye Center offers a number of workshops, tours, talks, and lectures as well as permanent and temporary exhibitions.

> *Address:* Alexander Hamilton U.S. Custom House, One Bowling Green, New York, NY 10014
> *Phone:* 212-514-3700
> *Web Site:* http://www.nmai.si.edu

ONCHIOTA

Six Nations Indian Museum The Six Nations Indian Museum is dedicated to the culture and history of the Haudenosaunee (Iroquois) Confederacy and includes a traditional longhouse.

> *Address:* HCR 1 Box 10, Onchiota, NY 12989
> *Phone:* 518-891-2299
> *Web Site:* http://tuscaroras.com/graydeer/pages/sixnamus.htm

SALAMANCA

Seneca Iroquois National Museum The permanent exhibits at the Seneca Indian National Museum include a clan animal display, traditional Iroquois tools, and other materials, as well as modern art.

Address: 744-814 Broad Street, P.O. Box 442, Salamanca, NY 14779
Phone: 716-945-1738
Web Site: http://www.senecamuseum.org

SOUTHAMPTON

Shinnecock Nation Cultural Center and Museum The Shinnecock Nation Cultural Center and Museum includes displays of eastern Woodland Indian artifacts.

Address: 100 Montauk Highway and West Gate Road, P.O. 5059,
    Southampton, NY 11969
Phone: 631-287-4923
Web Site: http://www.shinnecock-museum.org

VICTOR

Ganondagan State Historic Site   There are hiking trails as well as a replica of a 17th-century Seneca longhouse at the Ganondagan State Historic Site.

Address: 1488 State Road 444, P.O. Box 113, Victor, NY 14564
Phone: 585-742-1690
Web Site: http://www.ganondagan.org

Ohio

CHILLICOTHE

Hopewell Culture National Historical Park The Hopewell Culture National Historical Park includes a number of earthenworks built by the Hopewell culture from 200 B.C. to A.D. 500.

Address: 16062 State Route 104, Chillicothe, OH 45601
Phone: 740-774-1125
Web Site: http://www.nps.gov/hocu

Pennsylvania

ALLENTOWN

Lenni Lenape Historical Society and Museum of Indian Culture The exhibits at the Lenni Lenape Historical Society and Museum of Indian Culture are designed to educate people about Lenape culture.

Address: 2825 Fish Hatchery Road, Allentown, PA 18103
Phone: 610-797-2121
Web Site: http://www.lenape.org

PHILADELPHIA

University of Pennsylvania Museum of Archaeology and Anthropology The museum has displays of American Indian culture and artifacts.

Address: 3260 South Street, Philadelphia, PA 19104
Phone: 215-898-4000
Web Site: http://www.museum.upenn.edu

PITTSBURGH

Carnegie Museum of Natural History The anthropology section at the Carnegie Museum of Natural History has exhibits on a variety of American Indian cultures.

Address: 5800 Baum Boulevard, Pittsburgh, PA 15206
Phone: 412-622-3131
Web Site: http://www.carnegiemnh.org/anthro/home.html

Rhode Island

BRISTOL

Brown University Haffenreffer Museum of Anthropology The museum is home to almost 100,000 artifacts of native people around the country and the world.

Address: 300 Tower Street, Bristol, RI 02809
Phone: 401-253-8288
Web Site: http://www.brown.edu/Facilities/Haffenreffer/

Virginia

WILLAMSBURG

Powhatan Indian Village At the Jamestown Settlement, the Powhatan Indian Village portrays life in a traditional Powhatan village.

Address: Jamestown-Yorktown Foundation, P.O. Box 1607,
    Williamsburg, VA 23187
Phone: 757-253-4838
Web Site: http://www.historyisfun.org/jamestown/powhatan.cfm

Washington, D.C.

National Museum of the American Indian on the National Mall Opened in 2004, the museum's galleries and display spaces offer both permanent and temporary exhibitions on the American Indian.

Address: Fourth Street and Independence Avenue, SW,
    Washington, DC 20560
Phone: 202-633-1000
Web Site: http://www.nmai.si.edu

CANADA
Ontario

BRANTFORD
Woodland Cultural Centre Museum The Woodland Cultural Centre Museum tracks Iroquois life from before the arrival of the Europeans to today.

> *Address:* 184 Mohawk Street, P.O. Box 1506, Brantford, Ontario
>   N3T 4V6
> *Phone:* 519-759-2650
> *Web Site:* http://www.woodland-centre.on.ca

Quebec

GATINEAU
Canadian Museum of Civilization The Canadian Museum of Civilization has an extensive collection of aboriginal materials on display.

> *Address:* 100 Laurier Street, P.O. Box 3100, Station B, Gatineau,
>   Quebec J8X 4H2
> *Phone:* 819-776-7000
> *Web Site:* http://www.civilization.ca

Further Reading

BOOKS

Bial, Raymond. *The Powhatan*. Tarrytown, N.Y.: Marshall Cavendish/
  Benchmark, 2002.

Bragdon, Kathleen J. *The Columbia Guide to American Indians of the
  Northeast*. New York: Columbia University Press, 2001.

Doherty, Katherine M., and Craig A. Doherty. *The Penobscot*. New York:
  Franklin Watts, 1995.

Dunn, Mary R. *The Mohawk*. San Diego, Calif.: Lucent, 2003.

Duvall, Jill. *The Seneca*. Chicago: Childrens Press, 1991.

Ryan, Maria Felkins, and Linda Schmittroth, eds. *Abenaki*. San Diego,
  Calif.: Blackbirch, 2004.

———. *Narragansett*. San Diego, Calif.: Blackbirch, 2003.

Siegel, Beatrice. *Indians of the Northeast*. New York: Walker, 1992.

Trigger, Bruce G., ed. *Handbook of North American Indians*. Vol. 15,
  Northeast. Washington, D.C.: Smithsonian Institution, 1978.

WEB SITES

500 Nations Native American SuperSite. Available online. URL: http://
  500nations.com. Downloaded January 7, 2005.

IndianLegend.com. Available online. URL: http://www.indianlegend.
  com. Updated May 13, 2003.

Mashantucket Pequot Museum and Research Center. Available online.
  URL: http://www.pequotmuseum.org. Downloaded January 7, 2005.

Native American Sites. Available online. URL: http://www.native
  culturelinks.com/indians.html. Updated on July 5, 2005.

Woodland Cultural Centre. Available online. URL: http://woodland
  -centre.on.ca. Downloaded January 16, 2005.

Index

Page numbers in *italic* indicate photographs/illustrations. Page numbers in **boldface** indicate box features. Page numbers followed by *m* indicate maps. Page numbers followed by *g* indicate tables. Page numbers followed by *t* indicate time line entries.